Navajo Medicine Man
SANDPAINTINGS

by

GLADYS A. REICHARD

DOVER PUBLICATIONS, INC., NEW YORK

To the memory

of

JOHN FREDERICK HUCKEL

who loved the Southwest and did much
to promote a wider knowledge
and greater appreciation
of its native arts

Published in Canada by General Publishing
Company, Ltd., 30 Lesmill Road, Don Mills,
Toronto, Ontario.
Published in the United Kingdom by Con-
stable and Company, Ltd.

This Dover edition, first published in 1977,
is an unabridged republication of the work
originally published by J. J. Augustin Pub-
lisher, New York, in 1939 under the title
Navajo Medicine Man.

International Standard Book Number:
0-486-23329-4
Library of Congress Catalog Card Number:
77-73298

Manufactured in the United States of America
Dover Publications, Inc.
180 Varick Street
New York, N.Y. 10014

Contents

[iii]

Preface

To Mrs. John Frederick Huckel I express my sincere gratitude for the privilege of writing this book. It would have been pleasant in any case, but it has been made doubly so by the willing and efficient coöperation of Mrs. Huckel's staff in carrying out the many, often difficult, mechanical details. I am especially grateful to Fred Geary, who did the art work, to Harold Belt and to Herman Schweizer who aided in a great many ways.

GLADYS A. REICHARD

Barnard College
Columbia University

Illustrations

The plates identified by Roman numerals may be found at the end of the book.

Front Cover

Big Thunder (*Shooting Chant*)

I

Scavenger in the Eagle's Nest (*Bead Chant*)

II

The Snakes Assist in the Ascension (*Bead Chant*)

III

The Snakes Lift Scavenger through the Skyhole (*Bead Chant*)

IV

The Home of the Eagles (*Bead Chant*)

V

The Exchange of Quivers (*Bead Chant*)

VI

The Exchange of Quivers (*Bead Chant*)

VII

The Hunting Animals with Cornpacks (*Bead Chant*)

VIII

The Final Ascension of Scavenger Attended by Eagles (*Bead Chant*)

IX

The Final Ascension of Scavenger Attended by Lightnings (*Bead Chant*)

X

Holy Man Guarded by Monster Slayer and Child-of-the-water (*Shooting Chant*)

[*v*]

Figures

Explanatory Foreword

FREQUENTLY THROUGHOUT THIS BOOK the word "chant" is used in a very special sense. The Navajo religion will be explained as a form of control over supernatural forces. This control manifests itself in a large number of practical, magical, and religious observances. These observances are combined in a long and detailed ritual composed of many acts which must be performed in traditional order, and it is to the whole complex that the word "chant" refers. The word has been in use for nearly fifty years, and although it may leave something to be desired, it is as good as any to connote the complicated charm which the Navajo fervently believes is his guarantee of health and well-being, as well as his defense against evil. The ceremony, which may last five or nine days, is unified by a song sequence which may contain several hundred songs. These and long prayers, intoned like a litany, suggested the term chant, but it includes also a large number of other elements.

A chant is said to be "sung over" a person, frequently to cure him of disease, but also to bring blessing to him and all concerned, eventually even to his whole tribe. Purification, supplication to the supernatural beings for the honor of their presence, application of sacred objects symbolical of divinity to the body of the person who undergoes the treatment, the consequent identification of the patient (through the exact knowledge and performance of the medicine man) with the gods, and his subsequent absorption of the good for which they stand, are all essential parts of a chant. All of these are embodied in a long myth which furnishes authority for every detailed act.

Purification is attained through fasting, sweating and emesis, sexual continence, bathing and shampooing the hair in yucca suds, and vigil. By means of prayersticks, carefully made of wood and containing a tiny offering of something which the gods most cherish, the supernaturals are invited to come. If the invitations are properly made and deposited where the deity cannot fail to see them, it is compelled to attend. There are many objects which have been rendered sacred by the medicine man's acquisition of knowledge and the performance of ceremonies over them. These make up the chanter's "bundle," and when used in the proper way with songs and prayers—taught originally by the supernaturals, and handed down through many generations—will do for the patient today what they did for the deities in mythological times, that is, they will restore everything to a normal, healthful, successful, happy order.

Another kind of sacred object is the sandpainting, a picture of a scene in the life of the Holy Ones, made on the floor of the ceremonial house (*hogan*) by sprinkling dry sands colored with natural pigments. The sandpainting is an altar, but an altar composed of the representations of divinity, which becomes sacred in its setting after its placing according to divine tradition. When a person sits on the sandpainting and is treated by the medicine man who applies the sacred-bundle paraphernalia with the correct songs and prayers, he becomes the god and shares in all its miraculous powers. The learning of the chanter, which may take years to acquire, and his exact profession of that learning combine all the parts of a chant into an orderly unit which heals, restores, blesses, renews, and instructs.

A common order of the chant is as follows: On the first night of the ceremony the house is blessed and objects belonging to the chanter's bundle are applied to the patient's body with song. Then follows a long series of songs accompanied by drumming on an inverted basket. On the first day the chanter prays at dawn and sets up the symbol which distinguishes the chant. About nine o'clock a huge fire is built and the patient and all others who wish to participate undergo sweating and ceremonial emesis for about an hour and a half. Later in the day several hours are devoted to the making of the prayersticks. When they are ready, the patient (who should never see the preparations for his treatment) ritualistically lights the prayersticks with a crystal held to the sun and passed over them. They are then wrapped in a cloth. Then, holding the parcel in his hand, the patient repeats after the chanter, phrase by phrase, a prayer of invocation. The prayersticks are then placed by assistants in a spot where the deities they invoke may see them.

The performance of the first night is repeated on the second, third, and fourth nights, becoming somewhat longer as the ceremonial proceeds. Similarly the program of the first day is repeated on the next three days, prayersticks being made for different deities. At dawn of the fifth day the sacred items of the chanter's bundle are set outside the entrance of the ceremonial house with a prayer. They remain there to attract the gods until the sandpainting has been completed inside. This may be finished as early as ten o'clock, or not until nearly sunset. When the painters are ready for the patient, the bundle items are taken into the *hogan* and placed around the sandpainting.

The patient is then called, and sand from the painting with parts of the bundle are applied to his nearly nude body as songs are sung. Within twenty minutes the ceremony is over, the painting is obliterated, and the sand is carried out. For four days the same program is followed, different paintings being used, paintings of those beings for whom prayersticks have been made. On the last day the patient bathes body and hair in yucca suds, and dries himself with cornmeal which symbolizes future blessing. When the sandpainting is finished later in the day the chanter paints the symbols of the chant on the patient's body before he leads him onto the sandpainting. All this is to make the patient one with the deities.

The last night is given over to a vigil during which the patient must keep awake and listen attentively to the many songs which summarize all the acts of the mythical drama on which the chant is based. This vigil lasts from about ten o'clock at night until dawn of the ninth day from the night when the chant began. The patient signifies his acceptance of all the gods have done for him by "breathing in" the dawn, and then undertakes to keep awake until noon at least, or even longer, without engaging in any of his usual activities. After that he may sleep, but until dawn of the fourth day after breathing-in, he must not wash, comb his hair, remove any of his clothing, or do any work.

He must not touch anyone who has not been the one-sung-over in this or a similar chant, because he represents supernatural power and, for that reason, is dangerous. Harm would come to the one he touched because that one is unprotected by the chant. After the one-sung-over has bathed himself ceremonially in yucca suds on the fourth morning, he may once more assume his normal position in his family, but he is now more than normal, for at intervals he has been one or another of the gods. He has absorbed their power through contact with objects sacred to them and the painting on his body, and in case they might forget that he belongs with them, he has a tiny token to remind them. The performance of a chant over him has left him with a small but perfect turquoise and a small snaillike shell (olivella) tied to a short string. This he wears always on his person, and in case of dire necessity, he may detach it from his hairstring and, waving it before the danger which threatens him, such as snakes or lightning, intone a prayer to remind that danger that he is one of them, their child, their grandchild, as the chanter sang over him. His prayer goes on to say that as they cherish him, so he also cherishes them, and by the time he has finished, the harm will have passed him by, leaving his mind and body safe.

I

Introduction

JOHN FREDERICK HUCKEL, to whose memory this book is dedicated, was one of the owners and directors of the Fred Harvey company. The circumstances which led to the assembling of the one hundred twelve sandpaintings in the Huckel Collections illustrate the way in which his vision created various avocations and, in so doing, affected the lives of many persons. John Frederick Huckel was born in New York City on October 2, 1863, and was graduated from Williams College, Williamstown, Massachusetts, in the class of 1885. As a young man he had experience in newspaper work, advertising and book publishing. In 1898, two years after his marriage to Minnie Harvey, daughter of the founder of the Fred Harvey hotels and restaurants, he joined the Harvey organization with headquarters in Kansas City. He saw the possibilities inherent in the country and people of the Southwest, and it was not long before his creative imagination furnished inspiration for the designing and furnishing of the hotels and dining stations which now dot the country from the Great Lakes to the Pacific.

His appreciation of native crafts led to the establishment of Fred Harvey's Indian Building at Albuquerque where crafts are demonstrated by Indians direct from the reservations of the Southwest. The Santa Fe Railroad was so impressed by the unusual plan that it arranged for its transcontinental trains to stop at Albuquerque for thirty or forty minutes. The plan is still being followed as far as possible, and thousands of tourists every year may see Indians at work and examine the finest products of Indian and Mexican handicraft. The furnishings and exhibits of the Indian Building enable many who have never thought about Indian products to envisage their utility and appropriateness for interior decoration. The vision of a man consequently enlarged the purpose of what was primarily a commercial project so that it created a tremendous stimulus in the use of Indian products and a market for them, and at the same time pointed out to thousands of tourists a human interest in the Indians themselves. Fred Harvey's interest in genuine handicrafts has been a large factor in sustaining the highest standards of hand workmanship.

The Indian Department (which long ago expanded far beyond the confines of the museum and salesroom at Albuquerque) was Mr. Huckel's special hobby, and the ethnological knowledge which he acquired, combined with his literary interests, led him to write a book, *American Indians, First Families of the Southwest*, which has been a standard source of information and enjoyment since its publication in 1915.

Not only did his ideas stimulate others, but they had the effect of continually intensifying Mr. Huckel's own interest. Accompanied by Mrs. Huckel, he made numerous expeditions to the various reservations to collect pottery, baskets, blankets, and silverwork at first hand. He wanted not only to choose from the best, but also to base his choice upon close and exacting knowledge of his subject. This richness of background undoubtedly accounts for the spirit of genuineness which emanates from the establishment built upon it.

In 1922, when plans were being prepared for a new Fred Harvey hotel at Gallup, New Mexico, Miss Mary E. J. Colter, well-known decorator and designer for the Harvey company, suggested the use of Navajo sandpainting designs in the decoration of the lobby. With his wide knowledge and deep appreciation of Indian arts, Mr. Huckel readily recognized the artistic possibilities, as well as the unique appropriateness, of the idea. Thus began a search for authentic copies of Navajo sandpaintings which led to the purchase from Sam Day, Jr., of St. Michaels, Arizona, of an excellent collection of paintings which the Day family had been collecting for nearly twenty-five years. And thus also began Mr. Huckel's interest in collecting sandpaintings—an interest which led to the assembling of one of the finest collections in existence. To carry out Mr. Huckel's long-cherished plan—which he was unable to accomplish during his busy lifetime—of making parts of this collection available to the public is the purpose of this volume.

After the Sam Day collection had been obtained, selected sandpaintings were reproduced under Miss Colter's direction on the walls of El Navajo Hotel at Gallup, and the hotel was dedicated on May 25, 1923, by Miguelito and other medicine men who blessed it by sprinkling pollen and conducting such rites as the Navajo themselves use in dedicating a new home.

An ordinary man would have considered his purpose attained, but Mr. Huckel was not an ordinary man. He felt that additional paintings should be collected, together with the data which explained them, for very little information accompanied the first collection and it was unsystematic. Finally Miguelito and an assistant, with Sam Day, Jr. as interpreter, were brought to Albuquerque in the summer of 1924, under the direction of Herman Schweizer, who was made manager of the Fred Harvey Indian Department at its inception in 1900 and continues in that position to the present time.

The sandpainting designs on the walls of El Navajo Hotel were painted by Fred Geary, an artist in the Fred Harvey organization. He painted under the criticism of Navajo chanters who were much interested in his work. When progress with Miguelito and his native helpers at Albuquerque seemed to lag, Mr. Geary assisted them with their painting, always heeding Miguelito's instructions. Thus, in addition to his versatile talents and general art training, he has had the unusual experience of working under the tutelage of a great Navajo painter—an experience which proved of inestimable value when he undertook the preparation of the art work for this book.

Although he had agreed to depict the sandpaintings in water color, Miguelito proceeded with the task at Albuquerque very slowly. There can be no doubt that he had to overcome genuine fear of breaking a Navajo rule which decreed that sandpaintings should not be recorded in a permanent medium. Furthermore, it is a difficult thing for a Navajo chanter to paint or to give any part of his ritual without a patient, someone for whom the ceremony is given. A rite may be short, only a part of a large whole, but it should be given for a religious purpose, and a chanter cannot understand having it cut up in the way a white man demands. It is likely, too, that the strangeness of the medium contributed to the delay, although the painters seem to have mastered the brush and paint remarkably well. At the beginning of the work Mr. Schweizer made a list of paintings which belong to the Shooting Chant and as many explanatory notes on each as he could get out of Miguelito. Later when the chanter hesitated or balked in his narrative, Mr. Schweizer was able to check him by referring to the list and notes. Miguelito had a tendency to consider each assignment finished at the end of a day; Mr. Schweizer felt it necessary to return on the following day to the place where they had left off the day before, for he aimed to make the story of Holy Man full and continuous. By dint of incredible patience and persistence, he finally secured explanations, descriptions and myths of the Bead and Shooting Chants which, with some supplementary material, are presented here.

The legends and explanations were set down in simple English with many Navajo words interspersed. Since they are not comprehensible in this form, they have been revised, and wherever possible, the Navajo has been translated. Every effort has been made to preserve the spirit and accuracy of the interpretation, and if error has crept in, it is due to the shortcomings of the writer.

Miguelito was best known for his profession of the Shooting Chant, but he knew many other ceremonies as well, and Mr. Schweizer secured, besides forty-four paintings of that chant, five of the Bead Chant with the accompanying story. Up to this time nothing has been published about the Bead Chant. Besides the five paintings made by Miguelito there are four others collected by Franc J. Newcomb in 1938. These were added to make the series as complete as possible.

In 1931 Columbia University began the collection of Navajo sandpaintings which is now referred to as the "Bush Collection." Many of these belong to the Shooting Chant and in 1937 some of them were published by Newcomb and Reichard[1] who did not have access to the Huckel Collections. The Shooting Chant is, however, perhaps the richest in sandpaintings of all the Navajo chants, and at the time of the 1937 publication only representative paintings were reproduced. The Huckel Collection was found to include not only series of paintings entirely lacking in the Bush Collection but also full series of pictures which previously were recorded only sketchily. Consequently there is no repetition of paintings reproduced in this volume which will, in addition to supplying new themes, furnish also new material for comparison.

It has long been known that there are two important phases of most Navajo chants, one conducted "according-to-holiness," the other referred to as the "evil-chasing" phase. Except for brief tantalizing references, no published data whatsoever are available concerning the "evil-chasing" phase. Miguelito, however, had learned both phases and the stories which accompany the sandpaintings give considerable information about evil-chasing. Ordinarily there are two stories, one belonging to holiness, one to evil. The most complete performance of the holiness phase includes the so-called Fire or Corral Dance, really a synthetic review of all Navajo Chants. This feature may not be used for evil-chasing.

Since Miguelito was describing all of the paintings he knew, the story seems to include the fullest possible description of the holiness phase and the evil-chasing elements as well. The story of the Bead Chant is typical of the evil-chasing phase throughout and rationalizes the absence of the Fire Dance at the end, for it is not now sung in that form.

There are those who feel that the Navajo sandpaintings are in and of themselves a contribution to the art of the world and for them detailed explanations are not necessary. There are others who, like John Frederick Huckel, enjoy an exotic object more if they understand what it means to the people who conceived and made it. When science and art, both subjects essentially identified, are as closely interrelated as they are in the lore of Miguelito, they must be considered enriched by the availability of such imaginative material.

John Frederick Huckel died on March 26, 1936, leaving numerous monuments to his memory and, as must be the case with one of his vitality and force, many others unfinished. Miguelito died on October 10, 1936, and left as his monument to posterity his teachings which he had communicated as fully as his conscience allowed. Through the influence of the one whose background was diametrically opposite that of the other, a great gift has been given to art and science.

1 *Sandpaintings of the Navajo Shooting Chant.* Reprint edition, Dover Publications, New York, 1975.

Miguelito Navajo Medicine Man

MIGUELITO, who narrated the legends and made the original paintings reproduced in this work, was a Navajo chanter of great power in his own community, and was known and loved by many white people. During the last half of his life he lived near Ganado, Arizona. His mother's family lived in the region of Salaine, and he was born while the Navajo were at Fort Sumner, about 1865. He belonged to the clan Place-where-he-comes-out. Not much is known of his life until he came to Ganado where he married Maria Antonia of the Edge-of-the-water clan about 1898. Maria Antonia was a widow with a daughter, Adjiba, born about 1890. Three daughters were born to Maria Antonia and Miguelito. Atlnaba, now deceased, would have been forty years old in 1939.[1] Marie is thirty-eight and Ben Wilson's wife is thirty-three.

Like most Navajo, Miguelito had many names, the Spanish one by which he was known to whites having been given to him by Don Lorenzo Hubbell. As a youth he was called Stooped One's Son, taking his name from his father. When first married he lived a short distance north of Ganado and later moved to a place still used by his children a mile south of the J. L. Hubbell Trading Post. His wife's *hogan* there was directly under the red point of a mesa and in his later years Miguelito was known to the Navajo as Red Point.

From the time he went to live at Ganado until he began to work for Fred Harvey's Indian Department at Albuquerque he was charming, poor and undependable. He had no sheep or horses to speak of and he worked only occasionally. He was possessed of tremendous energy which he expended in "going around to sings" and in gambling, monte being at that time the favorite game. The family was kept together and enabled to eat because of the skill of the mother at weaving and because of the kindness of the trader, Don Lorenzo. As is usual with Navajo, Miguelito had many heavy debts. Of course Miguelito did not always lose at gambling, and he sometimes worked on Don Lorenzo's ranch to pay some of his debts. In those early days he was foreman of the ranch hands, and an excellent foreman at that, when he chose to work. Don Lorenzo was interested in him and worried over his profligacy. In the manner of the Navajo sage Don Lorenzo constantly but patiently talked to the young man, encouraging him to settle down. To the promising Navajo settling down meant learning to chant. Miguelito was interested in chanting and was a good singer. It may be that his lack of funds prevented him from starting formal learning sooner than he did.

When Mr. Schweizer, manager of Fred Harvey's Indian Department, began searching for someone to demonstrate weaving at Albuquerque, Miguelito's family was chosen, probably more on account of the skill of his women than because Miguelito himself had much beyond a colorful personality to offer. However, instead of continuing at gambling in Albuquerque (where one might expect he could have found worse company than at home), he began to save his wages. He worked for Fred Harvey for long periods of time. When he returned to his home on the reservation he began

[1] Atlnaba, who married Curley's son, had one daughter, Ninaba, who was nineteen in 1939. Marie married Tom Curley, the half-brother of Curley's son, and has two sons, Benjamin, now fifteen, and Daniel, thirteen. Ben Wilson's wife has had seven children, four boys and three girls, of whom six are living. Miguelito, who was a true patriarch, used to say, "My daughters have been very good to me to give me all of these nice grandchildren."

to pay off his debts and to invest in sheep. His investments were fruitful and by the time the Harvey company wished to take him to the San Francisco and San Diego expositions of 1915, he was so far involved with chant learning that he had to be coaxed considerably before he finally yielded and went. He stayed in California with Fred Harvey's exposition exhibits for the greater part of two years, 1915 and 1916.

Meanwhile Adjiba had grown to marriageable age and was very beautiful. It was customary for the Navajo, before supervision by white Government officials became strict, to take more than one wife. Generally the second wife was provided by the first, particularly if the first was an older woman with a daughter. Following this custom Miguelito married Adjiba. The family was in Albuquerque when she was about to give birth to his child. Although he had had many contacts with whites, Miguelito had not accepted any of their treatments for illness or any of their religious beliefs. In fact, until the day of his death, he remained firm in his own faith in spite of the unrelenting pressure of missionaries. Consequently he did what was natural for him to do. He took his young wife to an isolated place on the Rio Grande where he built a shade for her and sang as the Navajo used to do to aid childbirth. His efforts were however unavailing and the girl died.

Whereupon Miguelito, with the Navajo fear of the dead and a possible feeling of guilt at having taken too much responsibility upon himself, came for help to Mr. Schweizer, who by this time had become his staunch friend. At Miguelito's request he took over the burden of burial, one which Navajo always thrust upon a white person when they can. Mr. Schweizer not only gave the young woman a decent burial, but was the only person present at the funeral. Miguelito showed his love and respect for the girl by giving over all of her silver and turquoise to be buried with her.

Maturity, experience and comparative security, together with encouragement from his friends, finally led Miguelito to start on the long course prescribed for a Navajo chanter. There is a long myth with accompanying ritual called the Blessing Chant, parts of which are fundamental to all other chants. Not every chanter knows all of this, for it is very inclusive, but each one must first learn those parts which give him the general foundation of Navajo dogma, the instructions for his own safety and that of the persons for whom he sings, and the relationship of the particular chant he is going to sing to the entire body of Navajo belief. Miguelito learned this chant from one Mr. Heavy, from Chinlee, and more from Tail's Son. We do not know how much of the Blessing Chant Miguelito knew, but, if we are to judge from his thoroughness in the others, he must have known much, perhaps even all of it. He next learned the Bead Chant from the same singers.

He continued with the same teachers to master the War Ceremony, the most common of all Navajo ceremonial procedures, which is not classed with other chants such as the Bead and Shooting, but which has close ritualistic affiliations with evil-chasing. Its purpose is somewhat similar too, in that it is performed to drive off harm incurred by contact with foreigners, or enemies, whereas the evil-chasing phase of other chants is given to drive off indefinite evils, that is to say, evil incurred through witchcraft. Miguelito continued with Mr. Heavy and Tail's Son as his instructors until he had added the Flint Chant, sometimes called the Hoof Chant, to his knowledge.

Having started the series of ceremonies which emphasize exorcism, Miguelito next gave his attention to the evil-chasing phase of the chant called Waning Endurance[1] which he learned from Mr. Yellow, a fellow clansman from Salaine.

Navajo medicine-men have various ways of combining their knowledge and of proceeding from one chant to another. The first chant they learn may be chosen somewhat fortuitously. Perhaps the man who coaxes the novice into chanting is his first teacher, and he therefore begins with the chant his mentor knows. We do not know why Miguelito started with the evil-chasing phase, but it is not difficult to see why, once having started, he continued along that line for a long time. In order to become a full-fledged chanter it is customary to master four chants of the phase chosen.

---

[1] Called by Father Berard and others The Emergence.

After all, details differ while the fundamental pattern remains the same, and after one chant is mastered, the others seem easy and take less time. Consequently Miguelito went on to learn the evil-chasing phase of the Shooting Chant from Gray (Blue) Eyes of Lukachukai.

Gray Eyes was well versed in the holiness phase of the Shooting Chant as well, and having learned some versions of the evil-chasing phase—Enemy, Waning Endurance and Shooting— Miguelito began the course on those called "according to holiness," for singing which he was eventually best known. He then added to the evil-chasing and holiness phases of the Shooting Chant, the Male Shooting Chant Life Branch, which he also learned from Gray Eyes.

Finally he continued until he had learned the greatest and most difficult of all, the Night Chant. His master chanter for this was Little Lefty from Bear Spring near Greasewood. Miguelito had mastered all the lore and had acquired much of the paraphernalia necessary to the performance of the Night Chant, but had never had the opportunity to secure the required masks. At the time of his death in 1936 he was looking forward to a hunting trip to the Kaibab National Forest where he was to be taken by his friend, Roman Hubbell, to secure buckskin from deer ceremonially slain, that is, suffocated with pollen and not wounded. This was one of the many things which Miguelito left undone.

Although in his youth he sowed his share of wild oats, Miguelito had the qualities which make for leadership and authority by our—as well as Navajo—definition. Above all he was highly intelligent, the Navajo proof of his intelligence being the vast amount of ceremonial knowledge he was able to acquire, retain and use satisfactorily. It may be that a good memory is not a proof of intelligence, but his mind was also curious and questioning. He was always wondering about things, putting two and two together, and arriving at astonishing conclusions, which often seemed quite reasonable, based of course upon the assumptions and logic of his own culture. The conflict between his tendency to reason and the requirements of his dogma led occasionally, as is natural, to rationalization which in some circumstances might be called social intelligence.

He followed out his precepts conscientiously, but as he was not brought up in an atmosphere of rigid conservatism, he was able to see that certain Navajo rules decreed in ancient times must naturally break down upon the impact of a culture like ours. Consequently he allowed himself to be persuaded by his white friends, whose judgment he respected, to reproduce the patterns of the sandpaintings in permanent mediums. Roman Hubbell, younger son of Don Lorenzo Hubbell, who realizes the depth and power in Navajo religion, had always felt that unless someone did this, much that is best in Navajo belief would be lost as times changed and as young men became less interested in the religious lore. Just as Don Lorenzo induced the young Miguelito to "settle down," so Roman later persuaded him that it was his duty to leave his knowledge available for future generations. The argument was strengthened by the fact that Miguelito's three understudies had died or had failed to continue the exacting course required.

So it happened that Roman Hubbell persuaded the Chanter to record the paintings for Mr. Huckel, giving him specific instructions to do the best he could and to tell all he knew about the work. It has already been suggested that Miguelito found it difficult to draw sandpaintings when there was no patient "over" whom to sing. He had also to struggle with himself against the ruling that they should not be made permanent although there was precedent in the fact that the chanters from Chinlee had already painted some designs for Sam Day, Jr. Miguelito overcame this difficulty in the fascination of working with brush and paper, but in breaking the taboo other problems arose when they began working at Albuquerque in 1924. Mr. Schweizer wanted him to draw all the paintings he knew in rapid succession day after day. In even the most elaborate performance of a Navajo chant, except for the Night Chant, not more than four, or at most five, paintings are made. Consequently the fulfilment of this task was what the Navajo call "overdoing." And there was still another tenet to be broken, the teaching that no singer should ever "give up all" he knows to anyone at one particular time. Something should always be held back. One may return to it upon another occasion, or the novice may get it from another instructor. When viewed from the Navajo point of view, it may readily be seen that the old man had many difficult decisions to make.

His solution was the result of his essential honesty and rationalization. He was accepting a large fee for his compromise and should therefore deliver the goods. He had promised his white friend at Ganado to do the job. Besides, there was Mr. Schweizer checking him and daily spurring him on. He therefore took a chance that, by prayer and purification, he could atone for the sin of breaking the rules; and however wildly the conflict raged, he nevertheless made the paintings and made them accurately. Under Mr. Schweizer's friendly insistence he gave the stories which go with them.

The manner in which he carried out his difficult task demonstrates certain outstanding features of Miguelito's character, his bravery and honesty, and his willingness to face facts. He had made an agreement which he would fulfil to the letter, even though it involved certain requirements upon which he had not reckoned. He would trust in the power of his faith and the processes it prescribed to remove such harm as might ensue. That which is most dangerous according to Navajo tenet is the unknown error. Known and acknowledged mistakes can be removed by ceremonial properly conducted.

Miguelito boasted of his physical bravery with a formality which belonged to the era preceding the subjugation of the Navajo by whites. The greatest honor which could come to a man, and one of which he had a right to boast, was prowess in warfare. Since there was no avowed warfare after the Navajo returned from Fort Sumner in 1868, the only chance Miguelito had of participating in war was when he assisted the American soldiers in the pitiable raid upon the Hopi villages to take the children to boarding schools. This gave him the right of a warrior to name children, an honor in which he took great pride.

In my opinion he showed almost superhuman courage upon an occasion which he regarded only in terms of outraged anger. When the most heinous crime of which native can be accused was charged to him, he met the accusation in the only way possible to down it convincingly. Tribes which believe in witchcraft may make it a formidable weapon against even the most innocent, for witchcraft thrives on whispering and innuendo. The person accused may not know he is threatened, and even if he does, there is little he can do for himself since, like gossip, the evil seldom comes out into the open. There is, of course, one way in which it may be everlastingly overcome, and that is to face the accuser directly so that he is compelled to make his case definite. To do this puts one into the position of acknowledging that the crime exists, and force of personality must decide which is the criminal, the one accused or the accuser.

Since Miguelito's rise to power, wealth and fame was rapid, the accusation that he had gained them by foul means was to be expected. Some of those who did not share in his prosperity insinuated that his wealth had been attained at the expense of others. Miguelito was accused of having cheated a weak man out of his wealth, particularly out of his horses. There are far too many incidents strung through the years to allow an outsider to judge the right of the matter. Certain it is, however, that the "little man" always gave up when a situation became difficult. He was not even respected by his own children, of which there are many, and had no standing with adults of his neighborhood, although he got his living by moving from one *hogan* to another, each occupied by a family ever more remotely related to him, which fed him because it is Navajo custom to do so.

The man who told me this also said that Miguelito was suspected of having acquired his ceremonial knowledge without paying for it. This is a downright lie, for whites and Indians alike testify to the fact that Miguelito had the Shooting Chant sung over him in elaborate fashion and at the time gave expensive gifts to Gray Eyes. At another time he and Roman Hubbell shared the expenses of a Night Chant at which he paid off in part Little Lefty, his teacher. These are the ways in which Navajo expect and receive "payment," the public validation of debt removal. Since many gifts are given privately, there is no way of knowing how much Miguelito paid altogether for his learning, but that he did pay cannot be doubted. It is likely that Miguelito, who had a dominating personality, exploited the weakness of the aggrieved "little man," but there was no need for him to do it under cover of witchcraft.

Whether due to the chronic situation in which the "little man" existed, or to something more specific, in 1933 someone started a whispering campaign against Miguelito, the burden of which was that he ought never to sing again. This was spread by one of Miguelito's sons-in-law, but because the disloyal one talked to the others, it was not long until the rumor reached the ears of the old man who forced his informants to give him the name of the man who had started it. As soon as Miguelito found out who it was and where the man was, he hastened immediately to face him. This was tantamount to acknowledging the existence of witchcraft, a matter which gains its power from being hushed up. The forthrightness of Miguelito's behavior turned the tables, for the man, when he saw Miguelito coming, did not wait to face the music, but jumped upon his horse and rode off hastily, thus putting himself in the wrong. This incident seems to me to prove Miguelito's strength in the face of the most difficult situation a man can be asked to meet, and to show that his faith in himself and in the supernaturals which helped him was sufficient to meet the most exacting test.

In these incidents of the life of a successful Navajo it is difficult to say whether bravery, honesty, self-confidence or faith was paramount. It was doubtless a combination of them all. When I attempt to explain native beliefs, such as those of the Navajo, to those who hold other beliefs, the first question that is asked is, "But don't the people know the medicine men are putting something over on them?"

Never in my six-year acquaintance with Miguelito was there the slightest evidence that he was "putting anything over" unless the most exacting and conscientious performance of a minister's or doctor's duty could be so construed. The fact that the members of his own family whom he loved subjected themselves to his ministrations is one proof of his good faith.

However, when Maria Antonia, his wife, was desperately ill with pneumonia, Miguelito like a white doctor, summoned a Flint Chanter although he himself was proficient at singing the Flint Chant, prescribed because knives (flints) were cutting at her lungs. Miguelito had perfect faith in the power of this man to cure.

It is the custom for even famous chanters to call in others to treat members of their own families, a matter of professional etiquette which we can well understand. Still others, among whom Miguelito was sometimes numbered, believed they could do best for even their closest relatives. Miguelito may have called upon a fellow chanter to sing over his wife at this particular time for reasons of etiquette, but there was probably another cause. One night after dark during the winter before Maria Antonia's illness Miguelito came home much fatigued and dispirited, and related the following happening with its consequent inevitability:

"Something awful is going to happen! I was gathering medicine (meaning herbs) on the mountain. I had my bundle with its many flint arrow points with me, as I had to use some of them to cut the plants and twigs. But while I was doing so, I lost a flint. I spent hours hunting for it, but I could not find it and it must be gone for good. Something is surely going to happen!"

Various reasons were given for Maria Antonia's illness and subsequent death that summer, but for Miguelito the ultimate cause was his loss of the sacred flint belonging to his bundle. He tried to correct the error by having another chanter sing over her, but it was impossible to forestall fate.

I find this incident most illuminating in the interpretation of Navajo thought, but I relate it here primarily to demonstrate the honesty of the man. He was all alone when he lost the flint. The bundle with its contents was his, and there was no reason to suppose that anyone except he himself knew how many flints there were or would ever miss one of them. He might very well have done without it or he might have replaced it more or less surreptitiously. Instead he chose to tell the family about it, thus acknowledging his own part in the accident. It would be hard to believe that such a man was a wizard or was "putting something over" on someone.

Other occurrences demonstrate the sanctity of a promise, contract or voluntary responsibility. I was living in one of Miguelito's *hogans* when he started to sing the Male Shooting Chant in one of its most complete forms for his daughter, Marie. We white people always need an intermediary, and just as he served as one between the Fred Harvey company and Miguelito, so Roman Hubbell served for me. He talked to Miguelito who promised that I should be allowed to see everything I wanted to see about the chant, that I should be allowed to take notes and even pictures if I wished. This was in the summer of 1932, and Miguelito no longer had any fear of the written word or illustration. But on the very first day when I was busily taking notes on the ritual, a visitor with some little authority, but not nearly as much as Miguelito, objected, asking why "that white woman" was here, why she had a pencil and notebook, etc., etc. After a short discussion which did not become heated in any way, Miguelito asked me to put the pencil and notebook away. I did so and the rites continued without further interruption.

The Chanter was very busy during those days for he had made up his mind to perform the Shooting Chant in its most complete form and he had only a few helpers. Nevertheless, at the first intermission he came to my *hogan* to hold a little council. It was true, he said, that he had promised me all the help I needed and he had every intention of keeping his promise. But if one who was not satisfied objected to anything about the sing, it would make for discord and the sing would not be successful. That was the reason he did not want to argue at the time. At the same time he did not want me to think he had failed to keep his word. He did not really mind if I took notes or even pictures, but perhaps it would be better if I would not use pencil and paper, but just try to remember what went on. I could write it down afterward and if there was any doubt he could correct me.

Here was a situation which might have made for discord no matter which way one looked at it. The Navajo critic was certainly going to protest at the breaking of the rules. I might be expected to make a fuss because an agreement had not been kept. If I insisted, there was no assurance that, even though Miguelito talked down his critic of the first day, none would appear on subsequent days. I was only one and they were many. I could yield for I would not miss anything really and there would be no further danger of disharmony.

After this I could never believe that Miguelito was "holding out on me" especially after I discovered that the argument had been smoothly introduced by the man who had insinuated to me that Miguelito was a wizard. Because of these occurrences I am convinced that Miguelito's some-time hesitation in explaining all to Mr. Schweizer when he was painting at Albuquerque was due to fear of breaking a ceremonial law, to inexperience as to how far one might go in so doing, and to doubt in one's power of correction once a voluntary departure from rule had been made. After eight years of working away from home as well as under decreed conditions, Miguelito's faith in himself and in his power from the supernaturals was confirmed. He himself did not fear giving permanence to the lore, but he respected the feelings of his fellows to whom it was unconventional. I ascribe his compromise to social intelligence rather than to duplicity.

A quality which contributed largely to Miguelito's success was his determination, his ability to persist even when the odds seemed against him. Naturally this spirit of determination also gave grounds for some to judge him as domineering, as has been suggested. They were correct if the Chanter was confronting a man with no self-confidence. In order to be a successful chanter a Navajo needs endurance and discipline. Once he had given up drinking and gambling and given himself over to the supernaturals, the old man did so with characteristic wholeheartedness. If it was right to perform a chant so, thus it must be performed down to the last detail. There are a few whites on the Navajo reservation who have seen enough of Navajo chants to judge whether they are performed well or carelessly. For some years Miguelito and the chanters in the immediate vicinity of Ganado were my ideals and I thought all chants went off with the same smoothness and style. Later I had the opportunity to witness chants on other parts of the reservation. In comparing Miguelito's with other chants performed elsewhere other whites agree with me that his were done with exceptional authority and finish.

He was relentless in the detection of error. He was patient when correction was necessary and tolerant of ignorance, often softening his criticism with a joke, but he did not allow carelessness to triumph or an error to remain, nor did he tolerate short cuts. There are many requirements of a sing which are irksome to Navajo as well as to whites. One of these is the decree that the patient should not wash, comb the hair or work for four nights after the sing is over. In order to render my handling of "dangerous" (*i.e.*, supernatural) powers safe for me, Miguelito sang the Shooting Chant over me for five days; to the best of my ability I kept the laws. To fulfil all the requirements the chant should be sung four times. The second time it lasted only two nights, but the period of purification was the same, four days longer. A Navajo girl told me that her mother at a far distant point of the reservation had abstained from cleanliness only two nights and I advanced this as an argument to Miguelito as to why I should be let off sooner. He retorted, "Yes! Her Singer was careless. And you know what happened don't you? She was bitten by a snake right after that! That would not have happened had she done as she should have done." Whereupon I kept the commandments for the prescribed time!

Just as it is impossible to draw a sharp line between courage and honesty, so one cannot distinguish absolutely between self-confidence and conceit, or even separate them completely from faith. When a man has the courage of his convictions he is sure he is right. The question then is to distinguish conceit, which is individual, from conviction, which may be social. The distinction was borne in upon me once more by an incident which occurred in ceremonial.[1] The first time I heard Miguelito say during a chant "I know this sing perfectly and no one knows it as well as I," I put the speech down to conceited boasting. However, I heard it again in about the same place of ceremonial procedure from him, and somewhat less arrogantly, but nonetheless confidently from other chanters. In working over the myth, which is a dramatic and systematic account of ceremonial procedure, I discovered that a statement of this sort is a formalized confession of faith which may be expressed by chanter or patient, preferably by both. "Do you believe I know this chant and practise it better than any others?" "Yes, I do believe this is true, or I should not have chosen you to sing it over me."

In all matters, we as white people subservient to the culture we have built up, tend to interpret all behavior in terms of personality or individuality. The Navajo has much to teach us about individualism, but at the same time he behaves according to group tenets, and group laws are usually writ in ceremonial.

During the first summer I lived at Miguelito's ranch, lightning struck the flock and nine sheep were killed. As soon as possible, we went for the head of the household, who was about eight miles away. Within two hours he had been brought back, investigated the damage, removed the dead and, by incantation, the immediate contamination of the stroke, and had prayed for the safety of the survivors so that once more the ordinary herder could bring them back. It is not at all unusual to wait two days or even longer for all this to be done, and until it is, no ordinary person may go near the flock. Especially was this true in days and places when transportation was slower. As

---

[1] I risk the repetition of certain episodes (Newcomb-Reichard, *Sandpaintings of the Navajo Shooting Chant*, pp. 14, 16) because they are characteristic of the man, and because the accounts previously given are available to few readers and are only briefly generalized.

was his custom, the old man came to visit and smoke with me after the task was done. He then asseverated, "Nine of them died. When I got there they were all bloated. Had I arrived sooner I could have brought them to life by singing. It is too late after they are swollen up."

Was this conceit or faith? It seems to me not analogous to wilful boasting, but more nearly similar to the belief in miracles, and to the recital of cures by faith which are more often couched in terms which sound boastful than not. In the words of the believer, "I," the instrument of God, may take the place of the "power" of that same God which works invisibly and indefinably.

The Navajo usually however simply includes himself as one of the innumerable and universal instruments through which "power" works, and he is just as likely to assign efficacy to inanimate objects as to himself. This was demonstrated colorfully by an incident in Miguelito's career. In 1934 an officer of the Department of Indian Affairs was taking Miguelito, some members of his family and other Indians to an exposition at Atlanta, Georgia. One day the party had left the tourist camp where they had put up and had proceeded about fifteen miles when Miguelito announced casually, "We can't go on! Something terrible will happen to us!"

Surprised, the official asked, "Why?"

"Because I hung my medicine bundle over the door back there where we stayed and I forgot to take it."

Not wishing to retrace the distance, the white man suggested telephoning back and having the bundle sent to them. It did not take more than fifteen minutes to locate the bundle and arrange for delivery to its owner, but in that time the truck in which some Indians were riding broke down. This was the only untoward happening in the five thousand miles the party covered. This time it was the bundle, full of sacred power, which reminded because the man had forgotten.

A characteristic of the mature Miguelito, at times difficult to interpret, was his sense of responsibility. I have said that in his youth he had no sense of responsibility, a statement which would doubtless be qualified if we knew more intimate details of his life. It is more proper perhaps to say that such sense of responsibility as he had did not manifest itself in the ways we whites best understand. I can only interpret the matter as it came into my experience when Miguelito was a mature, respected old man. In those days (since 1930) he took complete responsibility for me as for the rest of his family. I wanted to learn to weave. It would be a reflection on him and upon his womenfolk who were expert weavers, if I did not learn. Never did it seem to occur to any of them that failure could possibly be due to some lack of mine. The same attitude prevailed regarding ceremonial. I was dabbling with "dangerous" things, things I did not fully understand. If anything unfelicitous happened to me, its cause would be ignorance. And who would be responsible for that but Miguelito, my grandfather, into whose hands I had delivered my well-being?

This attitude was manifest in all practical matters, and if strange Navajo did not treat me as well as they would other Navajo the old man's indignation was immediately aroused. And not only did his responsibility include me but it embraced my guests as well. One night a white friend of mine, fresh from the east and unacquainted with ways of living on the reservation, drove her car so that it tipped into an *arroyo* which crossed the road leading to Miguelito's *hogan*. Luckily no damage was done, but after the car had been righted, Miguelito came up to talk with us. The burden of his talk was an apology. "All summer I have meant to have that place fixed, but the boys have been so busy we did not get around to it. I am very sorry this happened and I should not have let it go as it is." And then, in justice to himself and once more to remove the blight of ignorance, he said quietly to the girl, "But you shouldn't drive around nights on roads you do not know."

My reflections ran somewhat as follows: "Why should he fix the road especially? It is not necessary for the wagons, and my car is the only one which used it regularly all summer. He knows that I know how to drive the bad place safely. Why then should he consider it necessary to fix it?" As usual my reflections ended in amazement.

Although Miguelito manifested this strong sense of responsibility to all for whom he "stood," as the Navajo would say, it was by no means limited to him. An incident which happened the winter after his death was one of many touching occurrences and a tribute to his memory. I had had the unforgettable privilege of spending six weeks on the Navajo reservation in winter. My stays, though lengthy, had always previously been in the summer months. A Mountain Chant was being performed eighteen miles from Miguelito's (and my) home at a place where we knew none of the Indians. Miguelito's daughter, Marie, and her husband, Tom Curley, accompanied me. Upon arrival at the scene of the ceremony about noon, Marie and Tom took their places near a fire around which stood various attendants. The sandpainting was just about finished in the *hogan*, and, after glancing about and seeing no signs of disapproval, I lifted the curtain and went in. On our trip back Marie said, "After you had gone into the *hogan*, one man asked why you went in and wondered if it would be all right. We didn't know him, but before we had a chance to speak, an old man, Red House who lives west of us, spoke up and said, "It's all right! She is the granddaughter of Red Point, recently deceased. He was teaching her to sing. He can't do it now anymore, but we have to do for her what he would do if he were living."

Miguelito was a good teacher. He enjoyed nothing so much as a rest, when he could hold a small child in the crook of his arm. One in each arm was even better. Each of his grandchildren born before his death had a special song improvised for it individually by the grandfather. When he was at work at home, the children followed him, watched him and helped. Never did he refuse their help. He always showed them how to do things and explained why they should be done thus, often illustrating with a story or song. Even with the smallest child, as with his ceremonial assistants, he did not tolerate mistakes. He often pointed them out by joking and ridicule.

When I was learning to weave, he detected at the very first glance errors made by Marie or me. If we excused ourselves, the fact of the mistake remained. But when I became discouraged with my lack of skill, at once he offered encouragement, "The first blanket won't be good, nor the second; but the third, that will be all right." When, after having displayed my first finished product to my white friends, he asked "What did they say?" I replied, "They laughed at it!" At once he remarked with indignation in eye and voice, "Tell *them* to make one!"

In the summer of 1934 the Indian Department of the U. S. Government tried the experiment of teaching a number of selected interpreters to write Navajo. The school was held at Miguelito's *hogan* with no equipment except a blackboard. Most of the native interpreters, although they were the go-betweens for Government and reservation Indians, had spent much of their lives in boarding-schools. They had little acquaintance, except a somewhat critical one, with the beliefs of their people. Miguelito was so interested in the school that he almost became a pupil himself. As it was, he came in whenever he could, and whenever we came to a moot point, we referred it to him for settlement. He not only answered our questions but volunteered much information which none of us knew existed. One day as we wrote the names of birds, he helped us to identify them, and as each name went up on the board and down in the notebooks, he quietly intoned the Navajo song dedicated to that particular bird.

It may be that it is easy enough to teach when pupils are eager to learn as were the students of the Hogan School, some of whom came at 7:45 in the morning, and none of whom left before five in the afternoon. But it is another matter to bring a stubborn untrained child back to the road of responsibility. By a clan sister of Maria Antonia, Miguelito (sometime in his career for which I cannot account) had a son. This son did not live near his father until he was grown and married, when his wife brought her troubles of neglect, infidelity and wastefulness to her father-in-law. At once Miguelito, aided by his wife and daughters, started out to reform the boy. This they did with all the means at their disposal. They encouraged him to stay with them and treated him so that he considered their home sanctuary, for his wife was a shrew. They also encouraged him to get work and to stay at it, often with negative results. However, although Miguelito might occasionally give him a strong talking-to, calling a spade a spade, he never nagged so as to drive the boy away. Most outstanding was the patience with which he regarded every lapse from steadiness—and there were many. With unfailing persistence he started the process of encouragement all over each time the boy failed, as strongly convinced that he would become trustworthy as if he were setting him on the straight and narrow path for the first time. Miguelito's son is by no means a paragon of virtue now, but the noticeable improvement, due to dogged unrelenting patience and tolerance, is nothing short of astonishing.

It is likely that training in chant lore is a reason that chanters as a class are excellent teachers. Since the chant is a long complicated charm whose usefulness depends upon the mastery of thousands of small details, a chanter must think and remember clearly. For example, a single prayer which might take an hour to repeat, must be recited *and learned* as a whole. It is thought to be dangerous to repeat a single word of it, or to make a correction, until the whole has been repeated. Furthermore, the patient should repeat it phrase by phrase after the chanter. If the patient errs or becomes confused, the chanter continues, indomitably ignoring the possibility of interruption. Training in concentration such as this must inevitably leave its mark, and if a man succeeds in practising even this part of the chant, the mind must be clear and the powers of concentration great.

Since too the chanter's version of the prayer must be repeated either by the patient or the novice learning it, the articulation must be distinct and understandable. This perhaps accounts for the clarity with which most chanters speak. They do not use abbreviations and short cuts but speak each word fully and distinctly, while at the same time they use a vocabulary far more extensive than that of the ordinary speaker, full of allusions and ceremonial terms. In all of these respects Miguelito qualified among the best.

While Miguelito lived I had sometimes asked Marie the why of a rite or ceremony and often she answered, "I don't know." Her father died in October and her older sister, Atlnaba, in April of the following year. Not long after I returned in the summer, Marie had a sing to purify her father's bundle, the one used for the evil-chasing chants; for it, like people, must be freed from the contamination of death if it was to be safe for her to keep. The cleansing lasted a whole morning for every flint had to be washed in yucca suds. Every tiny sack of buckskin had to be washed, dried and tied up again with its contents. Then I found Marie giving instructions to Tom about the direction of the wrappings and the kinds of knots. Her sister before her had had much ceremonial knowledge and had aided her father upon many occasions. Now I discovered that Marie's former "I-don't-knows" were due, not to lack of interest, as I had supposed, or to real lack of knowledge, but rather to the fact that seniors were authority and she was not. After the death of her sister she was the head of the house, and when I asked her how she knew all this, she said, "My father taught me."

III

The Navajo Religion

THE NAVAJO RELIGION must be considered as a design in harmony, a striving for *rapport* between man and every phase of nature, the earth and the waters under the earth, the sky and the "land beyond the sky," and of course, the earth and everything on and in it. In order to establish and continue this *rapport* the beings which dwell in all these places must be controlled. All of this rules out the idea of a single god, Great Spirit, God, monotheism, or whatever one may prefer to call it. In order to understand the Navajo viewpoint we have to reconstruct our ideas of religion and allow them to embrace things we have not before included, but at the same time we may not allow ourselves the comfort of categories or catchwords such as magic, animism, nature worship and the like, for the Navajo religion is so inclusive that it touches upon all of these, and what is more, in it each one of these overlaps the others.

There has never been a time in the history of mankind when medicine or curing was divorced from magic or religion, and the present is no exception. The South-European mother takes her baby to a doctor, but it must wear a charm against the evil-eye. Many denominations did not accept the law requiring individual cups instead of the single chalice for Holy Communion without a struggle, a fight for a religious principle. Vaccination is occasionally opposed not only by the religious, but even by those calling themselves doctors. The examples of healing by faith are too numerous to mention.

There is no fundamental difference in faith. Navajo and whites simply believe in different things. From early times Navajo have based their reasoning on assumptions which we could not accept. On the basis of these assumptions they have developed a religion which is elaborate, artistic in many phases, interesting, and to the believer, efficient and satisfactory.

One of the fundamental premises is the belief that nothing in the universe is for naught, but that the smallest entity has its purpose in helping man. Since man is only one of the infinite number of things in nature, he is no more important than anything else, a seed of corn, for instance, or a fly. But, in order to make his life on the earth tolerable, man must have control of that seed or fly.

The fly has "power." It can go places and see things beyond man's capacities, but so can thunder and water and the sun, moon and heavenly bodies. All these are phenomena of motion; but plants, earth and rocks have another kind of power, static only to a degree, power of endurance and rejuvenation. Since man has need of all these things, not one item of nature excepted, no one is more important then the other, and instead of establishing a symbol or a group of symbols which should stand for right, the Navajo religion seeks to embody all in a design which shall be mutually helpful. Consequently it follows that the Sun, which is indispensable, may be a "high god," but without the Earth Mother, the Sun's power, no matter how potent, would be futile. So far the argument is reasonable, but the Sun could also not do without the Moon, his partner (not wife), who possesses milder virtues. Certainly as far as their actual knowledge of the usefulness of the moon—effect on tides, gravity, etc.—is concerned, the Navajo could possibly do without the moon. However, the moon exists and in Navajo belief neither man nor Sun can do without it.

The Sun as the outstanding celestial body, and the Moon as the second in size, are powerful and man must establish a satisfactory relationship with them. In so doing they become persons. In addition to their supernatural powers they have not only human abilities to move, to eat, to enjoy, but also human foibles and frailties. The Sun weeps when demands too great are made upon his gifts, his wife becomes jealous because of his philandering. All of this humanizing combined with infinite supernaturalism keeps the most remote beings in close touch with the interests, affairs and needs of man. And, as if this were not enough, Navajo design is not satisfied with only one of any kind of supernatural being, but ignoring time and space, allows each spiritual being as many selves as it needs. Ordinarily the Sun is a mighty supernal human who carries the light-giving, heat-giving body as his shield, and when so doing the two are one. When his wife suggests that he pay some attention to his newly acknowledged Earth Children, he orders the Wind to carry the sun for the day while he stays at home and instructs his children. There is consequently the Father Sun at the Sun's house, and a sun moving through the sky on the wings of the wind. The story does not mention the fact—perhaps it is too obvious—but doubtless there was a wind-self who stayed at home as well as one who carried the sun that day!

The War Gods, Holy Twins, Holy People, or whatever one may call them, are even better examples than the Sun of the principle of multiple selves which allows for complete elimination of time and space. The two boys—in some stories there are two pairs or even more, and there are girls as well—were begotten of the Sun and born of Changing Woman, and represent man's contacts between the earth and sky powers. As human representatives they are Holy Man and Holy Boy; as children of the Sun and Changing Woman, they are superlative warriors, armed with all the powers of the universe. Holy Man is the Scavenger of the Bead Chant, the hero of the Male Shooting Chant; and Holy Boy, his exact counterpart, is Rainboy of the Hail Chant. It is quite understandable that an individual may take on different characteristics in varied settings like an actor in different plays, but this is not the conception of the Navajo. In the same drama (Plate X, p. 40) Holy Man, who cannot be distinguished from Holy Boy, is protected by his warrior-self, Monster Slayer, and his brother-warrior, Child-of-the-water. In other words, two figures stand for the impersonation of three individuals, Holy Man, Holy Boy and Enemy Slayer.

According to our reasoning this conception furnishes sufficient confusion, but the Navajo, not in the least confounded, identify Holy Man, again undistinguishable in two other paintings, with Rainboy who was "substituting" for Holy Man in a particular rite (p. 60). Still other examples are those of Plates XVII, XVIII, XIX, where four of the warriors are painted. They are Monster Slayer and Child-of-the-water at east and south respectively. Their partners, that is, those opposite, are Reared-within-the-earth and Changing Grandchild. These two are the same as their counterparts with the same characteristics and powers. They were creatures developed from the afterbirth of the original twins and why therefore are they not "other selves?" They *are* other selves. If the Navajo conception that nothing exists of and for itself, or absolutely at a particular time, or at a given point, is understood, the legends upon which the ceremonial procedure is based are quite intelligible.

The Sun, Moon and other heavenly bodies and Changing Woman are examples of gods, and from many points of view may be considered high gods. There are others belonging to the same class of which Talking God and *xactčé'óɣan*, Black God and Water Sprinkler, and Fringed Mouth are mentioned in the legends of the Bead and Shooting Chants.

The Navajo differentiate between "masked" gods and "Holy People," and in so doing confuse their own categories as well as ours, for the class of "high gods" includes Sun, Moon and Changing Woman who are not masked or impersonated in the Night Chant, the great dance of the "masked" gods. In the same class in Navajo thought are the Warrior Twins, Talking God and *xactčé'óɣan*, Black God and Water Sprinkler, and Fringed Mouth, all of whom are impersonated by characteristic masks and costumes. All of these, and some others which do not appear in the Bead and Shooting chants, are usually mentioned specifically by name every time a group assembles. "They asked the great ones for aid. Sun, Moon, Monster Slayer, Child-of-the-water, Talking God and *xactčé'óɣan*, they all came. And Changing Woman came too and the rest of the Holy People."

The Sun and Moon (and with them the Winds) are frequently represented in the sandpaintings, and not in the masked dance.

Talking God is also called "Grandfather-of-the-gods" and is their leader in the Night Chant. He is named from the fact that he talked in mythological times, although now he communicates only by his sound "whu whu, whu whu, whu whu, whu whu!" He has charge of the dawn, the east, and the chase. His most important function in legend and ceremonial is as *deus ex machina*, for he appears miraculously when the hero has reached an impasse and always has a suggestion which will save or restore. Talking God is the dominant one of the pair, *xactčé'óɣan* being the partner. His name cannot be translated and the Navajo do not even make an attempt at a folk etymology. This god has charge of agriculture, the west, and the yellow evening light. His sound which he emits alternately with Talking God, is "hahowa, hahowa, hahowa, hahowa!"

Black God enters somewhat incidentally into the chants which concern us, but he is of great importance, being the god of fire. He invented the firedrill and first produced fire. In commemoration of his part in the play, a sacred firedrill is kept in the medicine man's bundle. With this drill the fire used for purification by sweating on the first day of the performance is kindled.

While it can never be said that any member of a pair is the complete antithesis of the other, nevertheless some characters have opposite qualities. Water Sprinkler, who accompanies Black God, is an example, for after Black God has kindled a fire, usually by striking lightning sparks from his drill, Water Sprinkler extinguishes it. He has control of water from the sky and can produce rain, and he is considered the water-carrier of the gods. He too has a peculiar cry "yuh, yuh, yuh, yuh!"

Fringed Mouth appears with Talking God in one incident (p. 29) of the Bead Chant. Not much is known of the character of this god except that he assisted in many of the rites put on by the gods as a group or, as in this case, gave aid to a person hard-pressed.

Since the story of the Shooting Chant is primarily one of the adventures of the Sacred Twins or Warrior Gods (Holy Man and Holy Boy), many of their characteristics will be described as the tale unfolds. They are frequently depicted in the sandpaintings in various guises and the Navajo conception of them is quite tangible.

"The rest of the Holy People" is an inclusive term. Briefly they are all beings having supernatural powers and may include practically everything in existence. Nothing is immune to personification, and in the sandpaintings, plants, both domesticated (corn) and wild, are represented as People (Newcomb-Reichard, Plates XXI, XXVIII). The Holy People might well be considered those who in mythological times were able to help man in cases where he could not help himself. In those days snakes, birds and other animals could speak and behave like men, and to human powers, they added the supernatural powers which made them dangerous. Nowadays they no longer speak, but their powers remain for good or evil to man, depending upon how he receives them and upon the side with which they allied themselves in ancient times.

There is still another class of spiritual beings and this class once more overlaps the others. Bat and Big Fly are not generally referred to as People, but their powers, though modestly disguised, are incalculable. They have the faculty of being everywhere all the time. "There is no place in the world where I cannot go." For this reason these two represent monitors, beings who give warnings of dangers and hints as to ways of escape. Bat is conventionalized as the guardian of the frontispiece and Figure 6 and Big Fly in Plates XII, XIII. Big Fly is a literal translation of the Navajo name of a member of the fly family which really has a habit of lighting on a person's shoulder. From this habit it derives its spiritual character of whispering in the ear of the one who is suffering. It also carries messages from one group of Holy Ones to another. When those needing aid send unacceptable offerings Big Fly whispers a suggestion of what would surely be agreeable. Talking God and Wind often serve in the same capacity.

In the realm of holy things "holy places" must be included. Because a supernatural event took place at a particular spot, the locale becomes supernatural. The idea that healing herbs, rocks such as crystal and the so-called "mirage stone," and water from far-distant places or places difficult of access have power, is so potent that sometimes mere distance or difficulty is of itself a virtue. The legends constantly indicate that names are charms (pp. 39 and 54), for if one knows the name of a danger, it is as good as overcome. So it is with place-names, and in many of the myths the chanter takes an examination on localities, in geography as it were, before he is considered capable of performing the chant. The reason for this is that in the sky, to which place the Holy People retired after instructing man about ritual, the same places exist in the same relationship to one another as existed on the earth in mythological times. Their names in the prayers commemorate the drama where they were originally used and thus repeat and renew the power they exerted at that time.

Numerous attempts have been made to locate the sacred places. Two results have been prominent, one, to the effect that sacred names mentioned in the myths are localized so that the chanter points them out from his *hogan* as the tale proceeds. Another chanter, relating the same story and living at a place far remote from the first, is just as positive that the Holy Ones performed in his vicinity. Certain white people have been intrigued with the possibility of locating far-distant geographical points and have indulged in extended trips with various Navajos. Their experience is that the mountain or lake sought is always some distance, an indefinite distance, farther than the mountain visible at the farthest point the party reaches. The Navajo likes nothing better than a trip, and he himself always has hopes of finding the lost mountain, as have many other people of locating the "lost tribe." For these reasons I have used the names given in the stories as interpreted by Sam Day, Jr., for in most cases he did not write the Navajo name or, if he wrote it he did not translate it, so that I cannot tell which of two or more possible names is meant. This I feel does not matter much since it is impossible to draft a map of a mythological world.

One of the facts that has puzzled students of the Navajo religion almost hopelessly is the impossibility of drawing a sharp line between what we regard as opposites, good and evil, for example. The reason for this is the main foundation of magic: *what harms man will also cure him*, and in this sense good and evil are one. A being has a power which man lacks. Man therefore wonders at this power and his wonder or awe may become fear. But man is opportunistic and persistent, and he reasons. It is impossible to annihilate superhuman power even though it be dangerous to man. What better solution to this conflict can there be than to originate and organize some form of control over the dangerous so that it may become beneficial? The worldwide technique which converts the dangerous to the helpful is magic. It often does not include a belief in spiritual beings, but merely the belief that a carefully worked-out procedure will in itself bring about a desired result.

Although a large part of Navajo religion and the fundamental assumptions on which it is based are magical, the belief in the spirituality of all earthly and celestial things takes it far beyond the realm of pure magic. Nevertheless, the Navajo technique of calling the gods and gaining their help is largely magical. The belief that, if conditions and behavior are accurately repeated, a result once attained will also be repeated, is a part of magic. This belief finds no deterrent in time. A family which builds a house on an ancient deer trail to an impound may, in the year 1939 when neither deer nor impounds exist, be afflicted with the confusion of mind suffered by the deer in the dim, but still remembered past. Space is also of no consequence in this belief.

A woman, although she stays at home, must coöperate with her husband when he goes warring

[17]

or hunting by keeping certain taboos. No matter how far away he may be, breaking a taboo will affect him and his success. Similarly, when a woman is carrying a child, the behavior of her husband, no matter where he is, may affect the child, not only before birth, but even as long as it lives.

A way to overcome the uncertain dangers of time and distance is to identify oneself with them. If confused deer caused confusion of mind, the reënactment of the situation which caused the abnormality of the deer and the restoration which ensued then will now cure the afflicted Navajo as well. The Navajo religion is then a belief in animism in the most literal sense, that is, that all things in the universe are animated and endowed with power, and are therefore spiritual beings. These spiritual beings may become dangerous to man, but a complicated drama which reviews the happenings of the past constitutes a control by means of which man may convert all danger to supreme aid which will function for the future as well as the present. The chant is that control.

The number of chants is large and from their names it is impossible to determine what kinds of ills they are expected to cure (as indeed it is from any other means!). The names are more like the titles of plays than designations of diseases. The Shooting Chant takes its name from the fact that arrows, snakes and lightnings are its primary symbols. Since they are the cure they must also be the cause of the affliction, consequently the Shooting Chant will be sung for one who is supposed to be harmed by any of those three causes, nowadays chiefly by lightning and snakebite. But the ailments caused by these three are not definitely classified, and in regions where there are many or famous Shooting Chanters, most patients will try the Shooting Chant. Another common one is the Wind Chant which has many forms, even as the Shooting. Snakes and lightning are closely connected with wind and are therefore prominent in the Wind chants. If a Wind Singer is more famous than a singer of the Shooting Chant, a patient is as likely, or even more likely, to have the Wind Chant sung over him. Because of the sufferings of the Scavenger in the eagle's nest, and the consequent dropping of the moulting feathers on the enemy below, the Bead Chant is supposed to be used primarily for skin irritations. Yet Miguelito sang it for a patient who had no manifestation of skin disease of any kind, a man who later went to the hospital where his disease could not be diagnosed.

The name "Bead" is given to the chant because of the episode of the legend in which Scavenger gained control of the treasures of the Spider People which are thought of in the form of stones precious to the Navajo: whiteshell, turquoise, abalone, redstone and jet. The word "whiteshell" stands for them all.

There is of course a way of determining which of the many chants should be chosen. There are individuals who have the gift of "seeing" and they are consulted by a person who is unaccountably ill. The kinds of things they "see" are objects belonging to a ceremony such as a rattle, a prayerstick, or a figure from a sandpainting. Sometimes a friend practises the chant to which it belongs and the seer recommends not only what sing should be chosen, but the chanter as well. Usually, however, he knows of some lapse from the path of virtue which has been made by the patient and he can pin on this the chant most closely related. And when I say a "lapse from the path of virtue" I do not have in mind for a moment a moral failure such as we should mean, but rather a change in the normal order of life. It is not proper to be struck by lightning. If lightning has struck a person, or if he has been in a vicinity where lightning has struck, evil has contaminated him. He is out of order. Order may be reëstablished by the proper conducting of a chant.

When a woman dies her husband should not pay attention to another woman for at least a year. A widower of only two months remarried. He became quite ill. The reason was that he had broken a taboo. He was not obliged to leave the new wife or to change his life in any tangible way, but rather to establish himself once more in the universal order by having a short chant of blessing.

In the complex and somewhat indefinite organization of all the chant lore two broad categories are outstanding even though they overlap. Harm, discomfort, disease, confusion may come to a person in several ways, through an internal or an external force which may be definite or indefinite. Breaking a taboo, being struck by lightning or bitten by a snake are examples of harm ensuing from definite, "natural" or internal causes. They are all departures from order which any human may expect. They may be cured by a chant which belongs to the class called "according-to-holiness" in which the inducement of holy power and its absorption by the patient are stressed.

An example of disease resulting from an external cause is an encounter with a foreigner. In the old days this might have been in war, but contacts with outsiders were of different kinds, and even today too much influence or contact with whites may cause one to fail. The cure for this is a performance of the War Dance in which foreign influence is violently exorcised by the use of a scalp, mock battle and triumphant victory. The evil cast by foreigners may be definite or indefinite and the War Dance has potency against either.

The very worst thing for humans to overcome is the indefinite, undiagnosed, intangible evil, that for which no human or natural cause can be assigned. This in other words is witchcraft; it is worse because it is likely to be internal and means that a Navajo has turned against one of his own kind. Often the cause is said to be the shooting of a "witch object" into a person, as often it does not specify the person who did it. Such an object may be the weapon of darkness or ghosts, as well as of persons. They are thought to look like small, definitely described pebbles collected ceremonially from anthills, and the purpose of the evil-chasing chant is to drive away the evil so induced.

The two categories which, like all things Navajo, overlap, have the most punctilious ways of preserving their identity. In all phases some time is given to driving away bad influence. There is purification in sexual continence, in sweating, taking an emetic, bathing the body and shampooing the hair in yucca suds. Fasting is also demanded, but it is not prolonged. When the chant is "according-to-holiness" all efforts are exerted toward bringing the Holy Ones to the sing. This is done by making and placing prayersticks which contain offerings of precious stones, food, tobacco and water, the specific things most appreciated by the deities invoked. When they have come they are welcomed, sung to, prayed to. Parts of their bodies in the form of the sandpaintings are applied to the patient's body. Through his learning the singer has identified himself with them. Through his performance, and particularly through the many songs which hold the performance together, he identifies the patient with the gods. After the chant is over the patient spends four days absorbing the power which was brought. Bits of the sandpaintings have been put into his moccasins. These he must not remove before four nights have passed. Sand from the painting has been pressed to his body; the sacred marks of the chant deity have been painted upon his skin. Tallow, paint and a token from the sacred paraphernalia of the bundle have been applied to his hair. For four nights and the intervening days after he must neither undress, wash, nor comb his hair. During this time too he is dangerous to all who have not undergone the same treatment, and children and the impure must be kept away from him. They may not eat with him or even handle the dishes he has used. Someone who has had the same chant or one closely related "according-to-holiness" will be his servant during this time. And when it is over, he is impervious to dangers of the same sort forever. He is no longer dangerous to those not sung over but the powers who harmed him must fear him and at the same time cherish him. He "has become their child, their grandchild." He will aid and protect them and all that they stand for. This means that they will reciprocate in every way, that man and gods are one.

If a person suffers from intangible or undiagnosed evils, the evil-chasing phase of a chant may be prescribed. This differs from the phase "according-to-holiness" in that most of the time is spent in driving out evil, although there could be no logic in the performance if it did not bring good after the evil has been disposed of. Since evil from witches and ghosts comes at night, much of the ceremony, including the sandpaintings, is performed at night. Since the deities of the sand-paintings counteract the evil within the patient, most of the sand of the painting is placed under his bed every night instead of being deposited in a place where it will not be disturbed. Some of course is carried out, each night a little farther away "so that by the last night the evils will be so far from the afflicted that they cannot harm him." Under such conditions it seems that deity absorbs evil.

Much time of the chant according-to-holiness is devoted to the manufacture of prayersticks which are placed as invitations where the Holy Ones cannot miss them. Once having seen them perfectly made the Holy Ones may not refuse the invitation to be present at the sing. Instead of emphasizing this feature, the evil-chasing chant emphasizes the making of hoops whose function is to restore the patient to his actual self because he has been transformed into a coyote. The reference to hoops, coyote skin and the dropping of the coyote skin in the legends refers to this part of the ceremony which takes up a great deal of the time devoted to a five-night chant. The version of the Bead Chant which Miguelito gives in his legend has to do with this. The werewolf episode is included in the legend of the Shooting Chant. I have Navajo texts of the evil-chasing phase of the Big Star chant, of the Chant of Waning Endurance and of the Shooting Chant, and in these as well as in those here presented the coyote transformation is of major importance.

The above explanation serves to point up two differentiating features of the main branches of the chants; the difference in emphasis and the difference in symbolism. In characterizing the various chants within what we may call the two systems, the same general rules may be found. The emphasis of a Shooting Chant and a Wind or Hail Chant according-to-holiness are to induce the deities to communicate power to their "child," the one-sung-over. The two chants have different color schemes, different arrangements of figures—sometimes the *only* difference in the sandpaintings is in color placing and arrangement of identical figures. The chants also use different prayersticks, sandpaintings, and body paintings. The paraphernalia of the sacred bundle, parts of which combined with the sandpainting form the altar, are distinctive. In some chants they are set before the door of the ceremonial *hogan* to protect it while the sand-strewing proceeds; in the Bead Chant they are placed *above* the door. If, as in the Shooting and Hail chants, numerous features overlap, as the songs, the bundle of prayersticks, etc., the chants gain distinction by the arrangement of the songs in different groups, by change in the order in which the prayersticks are set up.

Every chant has a sound symbol, difficult to reproduce in writing, which is identifying. In every chant there is a symbolic series of sacred words as they are used in prayer and song. Each chant secures distinction in the fact that these words, although they may be nearly the same in various chants, are arranged in different order and there may be a different number in the series. It happens then that there is no one way of classifying any chant or branch of a chant, but that its characterization must depend upon the combination of a large number of symbols each of which may be varied *ad infinitum*. In Navajo thought it is the variation of the most specific details and the recombination which form distinctive bodies of power. Each composition, whether it be according-to-holiness or for evil-chasing, concludes in the same result, the well-being of the one-sung-over and all who have participated, the restoration of that which has been askew to the established order of nature as it relates to all Navajo and Navajo activities.

An attempt to describe all classes of the numerous items which go to make up the intricate composition which is a Navajo chant will require volumes. The legend carries along in dramatic form the ostensible reasons for the performance and explains the procedure, thus constituting the dogma. Two of the myths, especially those parts explaining the sandpaintings, are published here with the paintings. The legend is the part of the chant last learned by the chanter, and if he is able to remember the proper order of the details, he may dispense with the myth. In other words, although a man may practise a chant and be respected for his profession of it, it may be he has not learned the myth, or that he knows it only in parts. Of course the oldest and greatest of the chanters, like Gray Eyes and Miguelito, know the myths as well as the other parts of the chant.

Besides containing the drama—the literature of the chant, not the least of which is poetry—the plot of the myth forms a device by means of which the singer aids his memory, a rosary one might say, upon which the beads of song, prayer, prayersticks, sandpaintings, medicines and procedures are strung. Though it gives the singer added confidence and surety, he may nevertheless do without it, depending upon other memory devices for his lore. Another of these devices which, unlike the myth, is indispensable, is the song series. Every chant has hundreds of songs, which like the legend, but in a different form, carry the theme of the whole design. For this reason it is necessary that a man be able to sing.

The chanter does not sing alone, for he is accompanied by a chorus consisting of any men who may be present at the different rites of the chant. The responsibility of introducing the proper songs in the exact sequence rests upon the head chanter. Often the song-group consists of four, six, eight, five, seven, or eleven songs—the number varies for different groups—composed of numerous stanzas. Within a song there may be considerable repetition, only a word or two being changed as it proceeds. Again the change, in music as well as words, may advance in groups. Commonly, therefore, one hears the chanter start off the song vigorously as he wields his rattle, and for a short time he sings alone. Gradually however, the chorus, having picked up the burden, joins him. If the sequence is long and the words obvious—like the repetition of direction or color—the chanter may even cease, and let his helpers carry on. Never however may he relax his concentration, for he must know how often the repetitions have been made, whether the order has been maintained, and when to break in with a correction. Ordinarily too, after a long outburst of song, it dies down because the last song of the group has been reached and the chorus either does not know the next one or waits for the leader to take the responsibility of starting it off.

Many Indian songs cannot be translated because they are either archaic in verbal content or even consist of meaningless syllables. For the most part Navajo songs are a contrast to this condition. In word, as well as in melody and rhythm, they are meaningful. Words however are often distorted to fit the musical phrasing, and for this reason may be difficult to understand. The whole field of Navajo music is one on which there is little published information.

Still another large group of elements used in the chant is the prayersticks. The hoops referred to as symbols of evil-chasing rites belong to this subject. Every chanter possesses a bundle, consisting of a skin, hide or cloth arrangement as covering, which contains the numerous items of his profession. Among them are permanent prayersticks of various forms to obtain which he has sacrificed much time and goods. There is no end to the forms these take. The symbols of the Shooting Chant are the four arrows so often referred to in the legends and four "wide boards" which were not mentioned by Miguelito in connection with the paintings. The "talking prayerstick" is a protection for the one who must be transformed from the despicable form of coyote back to that of Holy Man. Some altar items of the Wind Chant are snake-shaped. Similarly, ideas of the most varied kinds are carried out in the prayersticks made as invocations to the gods. Often they are cut from wood, painted, and filled with offerings, but they may be composed of cornmeal to which herbs have been added, in which case they may represent hail. All of these are symbols, indispensable symbols, distinctive of the chant.

The sandpaintings illustrate differences in the plants used by snakes, thunders or buffalos (Plates XV, XVI, XXIII, XXIV, and Figure 6). In these conventionalized representations they differ in color rather than form but in practise they are specific for every use. Rare plants and those which grow in remote places may be necessary. Since the plants of the high mesa region inhabited by the Navajo have not been satisfactorily identified botanically, and since the Navajo classification differs greatly from ours, this too is a subject practically untouched in literature.

In Navajo belief the herbs have more magical and etiological than therapeutic value. Belief is more potent than medication.

Of the numerous technical divisions of ritualistic procedure, that concerning sandpaintings is among the most unusual and interesting. It is difficult for one who has never seen them to realize that the Navajo may spend hours achieving an intricate mosaic of dry colored sand on a background of dry tan sand all laid on a *hogan* floor, and that, after infinite pains have been taken, the first thing the medicine man does is to walk upon it, guardedly of course but nevertheless making tracks. The white man is further astonished, even somewhat perturbed, to note that the next move is to sprinkle ceremonial meal over it, so that in a minute the clear delicate outlines are obliterated. The Navajo calls the subsequent procedure "using" the painting, for the patient or patients next sit upon one of the major figures. Twenty minutes after the patient and guests have been called into the *hogan*, one can hardly recognize the picture. It is simply a smeary mess of mixed colored sand. To the Navajo it has become a useful thing, something beyond the purely ornamental. It represents the presence and assistance of deity, and until the sand has been gathered up in a sack and ritually disposed of, it is feared as well as revered.

The description of the paintings here published includes a designation of their kind, the particular occasions upon which they may be used. References are often made to "just little paintings," sometimes also called "prayer paintings." The last term is a misnomer since all sandpaintings may be considered to have a prayer function. All the ritual and song carried on when they are used is in the nature of prayer. Paintings which are smaller elements taken from the more elaborate compositions may be used in various ways and these parts are commonly meant when the term "prayer paintings" is used. One time when such parts are used is during the sweatbath and administration of the emetic. A snake or an arrow may be strewn in sand at each of the four directions around the fire and the basket containing the emetic rests on a small sandpainting. More pretentious paintings may be made, and it is to these that legend refers as being used on the first four days of the chant before the laying of the large paintings of the last four days (pp. 64 and 67).

When a five- or nine-day ceremony is performed the patient may not be, often is not, ill. More than likely he has been ill, has been treated and recovered as long as a year or at least a season previously. There are several reasons for this: a person may be too ill to undergo the entire ritual, or he may need it during a time of year when it is forbidden. In such a case the rite is privately conducted. The chanter comes, the men of the family lay the painting, the rite is performed. This painting may be referred to as an emergency or firstaid painting, and although it may be a full version of one of the simpler paintings (the Skies, for instance), it is not one of the most complicated. Some months later when the patient has recovered and the family has had time to make the required preparations the full chant with at least four paintings will be sung. Or if the chant was one which should not be sung in summer, the Bead or Night Chant, for example, it may be given the following winter.

The most complicated paintings may be made when a sing is being given to dedicate the new paraphernalia of a medicine man or to confirm some other part of his learning. In such case, the ritual on the sandpaintings consists largely in singing.

The use of the sandpaintings of the evil-chasing phase seems to me to justify most properly the term "prayer painting." These paintings may be simple or elaborate, according to circumstances, but after one is finished the patient sits on it. He holds in his hands the sacred contents of the bundle, and as the chanter, also clutching some of the bundle parts in his hand, intones the prayer, the patient repeats it after him phrase by phrase without repetition, omission or error. Sometimes these paintings are made and used at night. At other times they are made and used in the daytime.

Plate XXI illustrates an unusual form of sandpainting. It is used for one of the most dramatic events of the ceremony. On the fifth day of a nine-day chant as the patient sits near the painting a man impersonating a bear and another representing Holy Man rush into the *hogan* with the express purpose of frightening the patient. This they sometimes do so successfully that he faints. The two actors and the medicine man then set about restoring him to a normal state after which he is immune to harm caused by bears, animals which the Navajo particularly fear.

Although simple elements of the paintings may be used for emergency occasions, for purification or even for a ceremony for which little has been paid, there are always large and intricate patterns of which they are a part. The most elaborate of these are made for the showiest form in which a chant may be given. This dance has been reported for the Mountain Chant,[1] but theoretically may be a feature of many, perhaps all, of the chants in the nine-night form of the holiness phase. Our legend of the Bead Chant explains that, although this, the so-called Corral Dance, was given on the last night in mythological times, it was decreed that it should be omitted hereafter.

The performance including this feature may be given for curing if a patient or group of patients wishes to put on a big show, or to try the ultimate in obtaining power, and has the resources to do so. It is often used by medicine men to confirm their learning and display their power.

In every chant the last night summarizes all of the events of the sacred drama which have been emphasized during the preceding nights and days. This is usually done by song, many groups of songs being sung from midnight or earlier until dawn. The last night of the Fire Dance goes beyond the summary for only one chant, for in it a representative dance from *all* the chants according-to-holiness is put on. It is held as often as possible in a well-wooded place where at sundown a huge corral (hence the name, Corral Dance, literally ''dark-circle-of-branches'') is made, large enough to accommodate the audience and fires to warm them, a great track, and an enormous fire in the center. Another of its names, Fire Dance, is from one of the dances, easily the most dramatic, in which running Navajo bathe one another in the flames of the cedarbark torches which they carry. Another event is arrow-swallowing (p. 47), and others show the miraculous growth of yucca and the dance of eagle feathers. The reference in the Bead legend (p. 34) that corn is no longer so grown, and that the dance of the feathered beads should no longer be performed, is to events of this sort. It is possible that the Navajo once knew and used these features and that, having forgotten or lost the skill, they now attribute their absence to holy decree.

When the Fire Dance form of the chant is given, the sandpaintings have certain appropriate modifications, one of which is the representation of fire in the center (Plates XIV, XVI, XXII). On the fifth day of the chant, runners, specially painted and carrying cornmeal, pollen and sacks of ceremonial food, are prepared and sent out to numerous medicine men who are known as leaders of dance troupes. The purpose of these couriers is to invite dance groups to perform at the Fire Dance. It is a great honor to be one of the runners, and an honor, as well as a blessing, to dance in the great performance. This is the explanation of the meeting of Wolf and his band of hunters with Mountain Lion and his troupe (p. 33).

The number of sandpaintings belonging to the Shooting Chant in the Huckel and Bush collections alone easily totals eighty if one even allows generously for overlapping. As one becomes better acquainted with the ramifications and elaborations of Navajo religious lore he finds that the number of paintings used in many chants may become very large. Yet during the mythological performance of the Shooting Chant, given in its most complete form, only nine paintings were used. In a single performance given nowadays by Earth People not more than four major and minor parts of another, or at most four minor paintings, are used. A question therefore arises as to the choice of the few which represent such large potentialities.

The choice depends upon a number of factors. One is the number and kind of sandpaintings a chanter knows. Another is the paintings with which he has had the best success, and he tends to

[1] Matthews, Washington. *The Mountain Chant*. Report Bureau of American Ethnology 5 (1887): 379-467.

repeat these many times. Still another element is the consideration of the possible cause of the patient's ailment. Another factor is the form of the chant, since some paintings may be used only in the Fire Dance form or for installation of medicine men, some must be restricted to the holiness phase, others to evil-chasing. The choice of a three-, five-, or nine-day performance will be determined too by the resources of the patient. If he is wealthy or if he joins with several others who can furnish the wherewithal, the paintings having the greatest detail and requiring a tremendous amount of work may be used.

After all of these things have been considered and reconciled the patient's family or the one who represents him may choose from a now restricted number of the paintings suggested by the chanter upon consultation. The patient himself, unless he be a singer of the chant being sung over him, should not know what paintings he is to have until he sees them finished. Usually they are chosen from groups. One group includes paintings of general efficacy, such as those of Earth and Sky (p. 45), the Holy People (p. 60), or protective pictures like those of Plates X, XX. There may be a painting representing the Sun's House and perhaps one of the snake group, as well as one from the thunder or buffalo groups.

In itemizing the considerations upon which the choice of sandpaintings depends I should properly have mentioned the patient's resources first instead of last. It will be noticed that in every episode of the myths which follow much hinges upon the fact of payment. No supernatural being does anything for another or for an earth person without recompense. That remuneration may be in the form of an offering (in which case it precedes the acquisition of the desired power) or it may be as payment long deferred, as in the case of Bead Chanter who finally paid off his brother, Scavenger, with the beads he had obtained by somewhat questionable means (p. 34). The ants had to dun Holy Man before they were rewarded for their gift of healing herbs in the Shooting Chant myth (p. 71).

There is nothing in the least mythological or mystical about these incidents and the demands made by the powers. The payment for Navajo power and absolution from evil is the most realistic thing in the world. A person may not undergo a chant unless he pays in numerous ways. The first is the fee to the chanter which will be a definite offering of so many sheep, blankets, turquoise, or silver, either in manufactured form or in hard cash. This fee is not fixed, although of course it lies within a specific range for given purposes. The general rule is that the larger it is, the better the chanter will do for the patient. One can easily realize the advantages to the singer in the fact of indefiniteness. In practise he never considers a payment large, but only what anyone might expect. Furthermore the initial offering is only a beginning, a binding of a contract as it were, which assures the patient of the chanter's attendance. Later inclusion of particular prayers, prayer-sticks, paintings or events such as the bear-shock feature may entail additional payments. It is similar to buying a piece of machinery at a flat rate and adding accessories, in this case supernatural accessories of course.

If, on the other hand, a person who has little or no wealth becomes ill, he need not for that reason be deprived of curative aid. By some means the family, clan, or clan-group and their many affiliates, upon whom the afflicted has a right to call for help, will accumulate enough to make an approach to a chanter. He on his part, knowing the exact pecuniary condition of the patient, will attend for a fee which, though it may not exactly fit, at least in some degree approximates the size of the flock which stands for the Navajo pocketbook. There are two elements of this psychology which differ from that of our own physicians and surgeons: the first, that the Navajo curer is indefinite while taking all the traffic can bear, and the second, that those who pay *want* to give up all they can, which is not always the case with white patients. It must be said too for the Navajo singer that he does not tell how much he gets from one patient and another, and if his fee is large this time, he will not refuse to officiate for another group for a much smaller fee next time.

Once the patient has assured the payment of the chanter his obligations for a chant are by no means fulfilled. His next thought must be of assistants. These serve for the food they get and a share of the goods (blankets, calico by the yard, tobacco and even cash) which are laid in the ceremonial *hogan*, and upon which the patient sits at the last painting. The performance is public. That means that a large crowd of visitors redounds to the honor and blessing of the patient. Visitors are enticed by food as well as by the more intangible recompense, and it is the duty of the patient and his helpers to furnish good food and plenty of it. For this item alone several hundred dollars may be required, most of it in terms of livestock, flour, baking-powder, coffee and sugar. The labor involved in converting these into edibles is not reckoned. It will be returned in kind at some later date. Some people are noted for their willingness to help. Others similarly are known for their appetites and lack of energy—"star guests," they might be called.

I have left the description of the process of making sandpaintings until last, not from any disinclination or lack of interest but rather because of a deep feeling of inadequacy for such description. Sand-strewing is an art which, after years of witnessing, leaves me wondering and fascinated. It is one of those simple arts, so "easy" that it beggars description. It must be seen and then can hardly be believed. The Navajo "just" collect yellow and red ocher and a chalky substance. They collect the roots of certain trees which they "just" burn to make an ash. This is an art in itself. These products are ground and mixed with sand to give them body, for they are too powdery for use in the natural state.

Then the chanter and his assistants assemble in the *hogan* which has been cleared out and cleaned. The assistants have brought in a large quantity of natural-colored sand from nearby and have spread it in the center and smoothed it off neatly with a weaving batten. The background may be an inch or two thick. In addition to the original black, white, yellow and red, they have mixed a gray-blue from black and white, a brown from red, white and yellow, and a pink from red, white and black, so that they have altogether seven colors in small receptacles.

Since all of this is done on the floor, the workers kneel or lean forward from a kneeling position, or stoop with the weight on one foot and the toe of the other. They work out in the several directions from the center, more helpers working as the picture spreads. And now it is as if I would describe a man writing. He has pen, ink, paper. He sits at a table and writes. I may say he takes his pen, dips it into the ink, grasps it between thumb and forefinger and presses down on the paper. From this description, in which there is no error, one could not learn to write. Similarly, from description, no matter how detailed or exacting, one cannot learn to make a sandpainting. The floor and the background sand are the paper, the colored sand is the ink, the fingers of the painters, the pen. They take a small quantity of the sand which they hold in the small groove formed by the index and second finger. They "just" press this sand with the thumb so that it falls through the crack made by the two first fingers at exactly the point where they want it. That is all there is to it!

The painters make a tiny dot or line, a long unbelievably straight or curved line, or what they will, because of skill which lies not in the materials, the position of the hand and fingers, or in any other particular thing, but in the coördination of muscle, mind and materials. Such coördination must be seen—and particularly felt—to be achieved.

IV

Legend and Sandpaintings of the Bead Chant

EVERY CHANT HAS A LEGEND upon which its procedure is based. The legend explains the reasons for the various rites and aids the chanter in remembering the order of songs, prayers and sandpaintings. The myth of the Bead Chant was told by Miguelito primarily to place the sandpaintings in their setting and to interpret their symbolism.

Changing Woman, so called because she represents renewal of the earth as the seasons move, and rejuvenation to youth every spring, was born of mortal parents. She was the mother of five daughters, one of whom was Bead Woman. These daughters were all supernatural beings. One was taken from the chest of her mother, a second from her left side, a third from her right side, a fourth from her back and a fifth from her spirit.

Bead Woman married a man from the far west and had one daughter and two sons. One of the sons, the One-who-goes-about-picking-up-discarded-things, hence the Scavenger, was the hero of the myth of the Bead Chant. He is the same as Holy Man of the Shooting Chant and other chants.

The home of this family was called Place-of-much-wool, named so because there were many mountain sheep. It was near a tall rock in the north. At this place they lived on corn which ripened in four days. For twelve seasons they had lived there when they decided to go to Whirling Mountain. They were on the way four days. The first night they stayed near Round Rock, the second night near Rocky Pass, the third near Feather Mountain, and by the fourth night they had reached Whirling Mountain.

The day after they arrived the older son went off to hunt rabbits and seeds, such food as he could find. He came to a place called Red Point where some pueblo Indians were living. Two of these Pueblos took him captive. One was from a place called White House (said to be near Mesa Verde) and the other from a place called Blue House near by. They took the boy to the White House and the next day made him work for them. He carried wood and water and worked in their fields, working alternately at White House and Blue House. They had taken his bow and arrow from him, and they fed him only scraps. They called him the Scavenger because of this, but sometimes they called him The-one-who-is-rough, because he had become calloused and sore from the hard work he had to do. After he had spent six days at the White House and five at the Blue House, the two Pueblo men who had taken him captive discovered an eagle's nest on a ledge of rock.

When they returned in the evening they told their people about their discovery and wondered how to get the young eagles. Someone suggested, "What good is this slave to us? Let us lower him into the eagle's nest, and have him throw the young eagles down to us. Then we can leave him there to die. That will be a good way to get rid of him." To this suggestion the people agreed.

The Wind had been listening to these plans and took word to Talking God and his companion, *xactčé'óɣan*, who were at their canyon home, "Your grandson is in trouble. The Pueblos who captured him are going to kill him."

The two gods started off at dawn to the White House where the Scavenger slept. Faintly he heard "whu whu, whu whu, whu whu, whu whu," the sound of Talking God. It was followed by the sound of *xactčé'óγan*, "hahowa, hahowa, hahowa, hahowa," just a little louder, and when *xactčé'óγan* spoke the last time the Scavenger looked up and saw the pair standing before him.

"Are you asleep, grandchild?" they called. "No, I am awake, grandfather," he answered. "Get up, then! We have something to tell you.

"Today the men who have made you a slave are going to let you down into the eagle's nest where there are two young eagles. Do not refuse to do this. Submit, but when you get there, don't throw the young eagles down to them. If you do, the Pueblos will leave you there to die and dry up. Let them pull the basket up empty, but don't be afraid. We will save you." Then they went back to their home in the canyon.

The Pueblos assembled and the leaders said, "Let's hurry before the day becomes hot." Before they started they had a great feast. This time they invited Scavenger to eat with them, to eat heartily, and he did so. The conspirators had made a basket of willows. Those from White House took the boy to the foot of the rock. There various kinds of herbs grew, so-called Black Medicine, Pink Medicine, White Medicine and Variegated Medicine. The Variegated Medicine glistens. The medicines were all people who spoke to Scavenger and warned him not to throw the eagles down.

The Pueblos from the Blue House took the boy up to the top of the rock, put him into the basket and let him down on the ledge of rock with a rope made of yucca. After he had landed, he let them pull the basket up and then refused to throw the young eagles down. The rock shelf was quite long. The young eagles retreated as far as they could on the ledge of rock, leaving the boy in sole possession of the nest. All day long the people begged him to throw the eagles down. At first the White House people called from below and the Blue House people from above. Then the Blue House people went down and they all coaxed him, but he refused. By evening they had used up all their water and became hungry and thirsty and they left, making no move to save the boy.

Scavenger found in the nest a prairie dog which the old eagles had brought as food for their young. The nest was made of hard wood and he made a fire by rubbing a piece of this against a dry yucca stem. He cooked the prairie dog on this fire. The Butterfly People came and asked him to go with them, but Big Fly came to him, told him not to go, and gave him the names of the two small eagles, once more warning him not to throw the birds down.

Finally the parent birds came back and called the boy by the two names of their young. They too begged him not to destroy the children. Then the young eagles came back to the nest. They took up their position one on each side of him, covered him with their wings and kept him warm all night.

At dawn the parent eagles returned bringing cooked corn suspended in packets from their bodies and water in hollow reeds tied to their tails. They also brought a yellow dish. They thanked Scavenger for sparing their young and fed him the kind of food humans eat. They brought a rabbit for their children. All day they could hear the Pueblos below giving their war cry and begging for the young eagles. This went on for several days. The second day the parent eagles brought a mountain sheep for the young ones and the third day a young antelope. Never did they neglect the boy but gave him plenty of cooked food and water.

PLATE I. *Scavenger in the Eagle's Nest:* The first painting depicts the scene of Scavenger in the nest of the eagles. The large blue circle is the house, blue because it is in the sky. The black line around it represents darkness; the white is dawn or morning light; the yellow, evening light; and the red, protection from danger.

Within the circle Scavenger is shown with the accouterments which distinguish him throughout the chant. His head is to the east, as in most linear figures of Navajo sandpaintings. The boy has the long conventionalized body distinctive of persons. The feet and legs are like most figures of people with the joints of ankle, knee, wrists, shown by red-blue, *i.e.*, rainbow lines. The skirt with tassels is conventional. The pattern on the skirt and the belt or pouch at the side of the figure may be varied to suit the whim of the painter. Miguelito customarily made these very elaborat e

The shape of the body, the feet and legs, skirt, belt, arms and neck are not distinctive. They might well represent any of the "people." But the color of the body and its markings, the face painted white, the headdress, and the objects held in the hands are characteristic of the Bead Chant. The body is black to show the black mist of the cloud in which the boy was enveloped for his ascension to the sky. The white lines crossing the body, from each of which four white lines tipped with red depend, indicate whiteshell which is symbolical of all valuable stones: turquoise, white-shell, abalone, jet, redstone. The end of the myth explains why the boy should be "dressed" with these. It was because he secured valuables of this sort from the Spider People who had harmed him.

This boy always has a white face—eyes and mouth are conventional—but the face is further distinguished by the so-called "eagle marks" on each cheek. It will be noted that they are made just like the eyes of the eagles.

The objects in the boy's hands are wands made of reed which were given him by Talking God and Fringed Mouth (see p. 29). The chanter keeps wands of this kind in his bundle.

The headdress is one of the symbols of the Bead Chant. The red part represents the bonnet which formerly belonged to the daughter of the pueblo chief, one of the items Scavenger and his brother took from their enemies as a punishment for the cruelty of the Pueblos. Mythologically it was made of red feathers, was given to the Sun after the division of the spoils in skyland, and now represents the red afterglow of sunset. Actually it is made nowadays of fine red wool or horse-hair strings. It is used in chants other than the Bead (which may not be represented in the Corral Dance, see p. 36) as e.g., the Shooting Chant, to represent the late sunset rays, and is worn at the Fire Dance event.

The arrangement of feathers on top of the red bonnet is composed of three eagle down feathers, one eagle tail feather, and a feather from the tail of the yellow-tailed hawk. They are bound together and held on with a string made of bulrush fiber. Other figures, such as the Hunters of Plates V, VI, VII, and the Rainbow of Plate VII also wear this symbol, and it is shown at the feet of Scavenger in Plate VIII.

The two birds in the circle (nest) with Scavenger are the young eagles. The tail feathers are put together with elements which represent reed tubes of water which the birds brought for Scavenger. The small birds are only lesser editions of the parents which hover outside the nest. The white rectangular marks on the wings distinguish the bald-headed eagle.

The figure at the southeast is the Big Fly; that at the southwest, butterfly; the red bird at the northwest is the black-tailed swallow, painted red because it boded evil to Scavenger. The yellow bowl in which food was placed for Scavenger is represented by the circle at the northeast. All these are inside the circle, that is, the eagle's nest.

The basketlike affair at the northeast of the circle represents the willow basket by means of which Scavenger was lowered into the nest. The myth has it that it was lowered on a yucca rope; here it has a red-blue handle, indicating a rain streamer.

The animals of the four directions outside the nest are indicative of the food that was used during Scavenger's stay in the eagle's nest: at the east, the antelope brought by the eagles for their children; at the south, a mountain sheep (although it lacks horns); at the west, the prairie dog which the boy used for his first meal; at the north, a rabbit brought for the eaglets. Joints of the animals, like those of people, are shown by red-blue (sundog) lines. The peculiar stiff lines running from mouth to heart are life lines.

The third morning the Pueblos brought many valuables of all kinds: beads, buckskins, food, baskets, and with them tried to bribe Scavenger to throw down the eagles, but he steadily refused. By noon they had become very angry and they tied torches made of cedarbark to arrows, lighted them and shot them into the nest, setting it on fire. There was room for Scavenger and his young eagle friends to retreat far back on the rock shelf and they escaped harm.

Just before sunset the male eaglet flew out from the ledge, described a small circle and returned. Twice it did this, then the female eaglet did likewise. The shed feathers of the young birds fell off onto the enemies below and wherever they touched the skin caused irritation like the sting of ants, and the people ran away. The irritation developed into sores as a punishment for the suffering the Pueblos had caused Scavenger and the young eagles.

At dawn of the fourth day forty-eight (twenty-four are sometimes used) eagles and hawks (which are considered the same) came down from the sky to get Scavenger. There was a group of bald-headed eagles, another of yellow-tailed hawks, one of big blue hawks, one of white hawks, one of large black hawks, and one of eagles half white and half black. They brought with them a turquoise basket and a basket of whiteshell in which to carry the eaglets.

The old eagles fed the Scavenger, painted his face with white clay and wrapped him in a black cloud. They supported him for carrying with three bands of lightning and three rainbows extending from the cloud to the eagles. As they started to ascend the eagles and their boy sang a song. When the Pueblos heard the song they surmised that someone must be aiding the boy and abetting him in his refusal to throw down the eaglets.

The eagles had some difficulty in starting up with their burden. When they attempted to lift him, he spun around and they could not rise with him. Wind took the news to Fringed Mouth, a god who lived at Red Rock. He came with Talking God. Everything was dark inside the cloud where the Scavenger had been hidden. They put a large crystal inside to furnish light and a yellow tube of reed to give him air. Whenever the air blew through this tube there was a whistling sound. The gods placed on his head the headdress of Fringed Mouth and in his hands a wand of reed.

With all these preparations the eagles were now able to rise with their burden. After circling four times they stopped to rest, made four more circles, rested, until altogether they had made twelve circles. They were very near the sky when they became unduly tired, for the moisture from the cloud in which the Scavenger was wrapped had dampened their wings. In spite of their best efforts they could make no further progress and finally black hawk and blue hawk let go and flew through a hole in the sky to where the snakes lived. They asked the black and the blue arrow-snakes to come down and help them but the snakes were afraid they would fall down to the earth. "You have wings and the power of flight and yet you cannot manage to get him up here. How do you expect us to do it?" they asked.

But the hawks begged until the snakes agreed to help if the birds would give up some of their feathers. The black hawk gave the black snake four of his feathers and the blue hawk gave four of his feathers to the blue snake. Then the snakes said, "Go back and we will soon be there. But when you see us coming you must all let go of the Scavenger."

PLATE II. *The Snakes Assist in the Ascension:* This picture shows the eagles assisted by the snakes. The snakes are angular and have on their bodies marks distinctive of the chant, a small square, the snakes' house, and the two parallel lines or "eagle marks."

In book position figures seem to be lying on their sides. It must be remembered that sand-paintings are laid on the floor, and the audience looks down on them so that they are always in position.

This picture was explained by Louis Nez of White Cone and there are slight differences between his explanation and that of the myth. If the birds of the story who gave the feathers were consistent with the painting, it would read: "The bald-headed eagle gave the black snake four of his feathers, the blue hawk gave the blue snake four of his, the yellow-tailed hawk gave the yellow snake four of his, and the black and white hawk gave the white snake four of his feathers." The discrepancy is slight. It may be that Miguelito described a scene with only two snakes, that Louis Nez indicated more, a change which is common enough.

The Rainbow goddess has the face and headfeather used in the Eagle Chant, a chant closely related to the Bead, the pictures of which are similar in many respects. Louis Nez insisted however that this picture belonged to the Bead Chant, but would be changed slightly for the Eagle.

Many sandpaintings have two small guardians at the east. In this case they are bald-headed eagle and black and white hawk.

Soon the birds heard the snakes coming and let go of their burden. The black snake crossed from the right side and put his head up over Scavenger's left shoulder and the blue snake darted across from the left putting his head on the boy's right shoulder; thus they succeeded in carrying him through the sky hole.

PLATE III. *The Snakes Lift Scavenger through the Skyhole:* In this painting we have an illustration of the subtle variation the Navajo make on a single theme. The boy is depicted as a person as in Plate I. He has the wands given him by Talking God and Fringed Mouth in his hands.

The birds helping him are in groups of four at each side of the hero. From east to west, the groups represent: bald-headed eagles, yellow-tailed hawks, big blue hawks, white hawks (pink here since pink and white are interchangeable), big black hawks, and black and white eagles. The yellow rectangles on their bodies represent packets of cooked food, and their tails are composed of reeds filled with fresh water for their earth visitor.

The element which gives this painting distinction and originality is the introduction and arrangement of the peculiar bird-snake figures. The description of the legend is identical with the picture. The combination of snake body with lines running down it, the peculiar appendages at the angles of the body, and the birdhead show the coöperation of snake, lightning and bird power, all of which were necessary to lift the heavy human through the last distance between earth and sky after pure bird power had failed. This picture was used for the mural at the top of the stairs at El Navajo Hotel.

In the land of the sky the house of the bald-headed eagles stood white and beautiful at the east. The blue house of the blue hawks was at the south; the yellow house of the yellow-tailed hawks was at the west. All were beautiful, but at the north a black house, the home of various hawks and eagles which had not helped Scavenger, was ugly. The houses surrounded a plaza in which there was a spring. Scavenger spent the night in the white house.

PLATE IV. *The Home of the Eagles:* The description of the home of the eagles is according to Navajo convention, but the arrangement of the colors in the picture is consistent only with the rule that black and white are often paired, as are blue and yellow. Their arrangement does not fit the usual directional pattern of the chant which is black, blue, yellow, white. Black and yellow are dominant (male) colors in this chant; blue and white are secondary (female).

Two "houses" are represented together, each pair surrounded with a rainbow. The designs at the east corners, white with yellow outline for one pair, yellow with white outline for the other, are corn ears representing plenty.

The birds are once more arranged as in Plate III, bald-headed eagle at the southside of the east, then yellow-tailed hawk, blue hawk, white eagle (in this case as in Plate III painted in pink), the large black hawk, and the black and white hawk. These are ranged symmetrically around the houses, making us read the circuit at the north in an anti-sunwise direction. This together with the color arrangement of the houses, unless we accept unconditionally the color pairing, makes the picture, though simple, unusual.

The encircling element is a rope of rain, not often used. It differs from the rainbow garland in not having white around and between the red and blue, and it lacks bunches of feathers at the corners.

Preoccupied as the Navajo are with water it is difficult to understand why the spring in the plaza which the houses surrounded was not represented.

The eagles were obliged to go to the earth for food. They returned with rabbits, prairie dogs and small game, which by means of prayer and magic they were able to turn into deer, antelope and other rare game. The eagles told Scavenger to cook some beans and corn to be ready for them when they would return hungry, and at the same time warned him not to leave the house for any purpose whatsoever during their absence. However he ran out of water and casually went out to the spring to fetch some. As he was carrying the water back the children of Black Eagle and Turkey

Buzzard saw him and reported to the inhabitants of the black house that a human being from the earth was there. Whereupon Turkey Buzzard shot him with turquoise arrows and Black Eagle with arrows of whiteshell.

When the eagles returned from their trip to the earth they found corn and beans burned and Scavenger lying helpless. The turquoise arrows had entered his foot and hip, the whiteshell arrows were in his back and in the back of his head. Then the eagles consulted amongst themselves, "What shall we do? Talking God will never forgive us if anything happens to him and he does not return to earth. What shall we offer the black eagles to have them withdraw their arrows and bring him back to life?"

They decided to offer buckskins and other valuables, but they were refused. Four different times the eagles approached; each time they were refused. Finally Big Fly, who had silently watched all that went on, volunteered in a whisper, "Offer just a small piece of venison and a roll of tobacco. That will satisfy them."

The eagles tried this suggestion. Black Eagle received the tobacco, flew in a circle, then placed it on his foot, showing his acceptance. He looked up at Big Fly and said, "You told on me! Otherwise they would not have known what to offer." Big Fly answered, "No, I didn't. They guessed it themselves." Black Eagle then told them to make a certain sandpainting and gave instructions how to make it. They did so, and when it was finished Black Eagle came back and, being satisfied, withdrew his own arrows and those of Turkey Buzzard. Then Scavenger was restored to life.

The legend here says only "They made a certain sandpainting," and does not indicate which one was learned at this time.

The next day when they went hunting the eagles told Scavenger not to touch the little blue waterjars that were hanging all around the house. Curiosity got the better of him and he opened them, causing it to rain very hard on the earth. Frightened because he could not stop the rain, he ran away. He came to Spider's house. Spider wove a web around him and drew him helpless up to the ceiling. The eagles hunted for him and tracked him to Spider's home where they found the boy held captive in a web. They went back and called Black God, the god of fire, and he went to Spider's house. Spider told him to get out but he was not afraid and would not leave. He asked where his grandchild was, but Spider said he did not know. "I have not seen him. Now get away from here and don't come around here any more," said Spider to Black God. Then Black God threatened, "If you don't tell me where he is, I am going to burn your house."

Spider pleaded with him not to do that but he said, "Since you are deceiving me, I shall not listen to your plea."

Black God took out his firedrill and twirled it. The fourth time he spun it the strings of the web which bound Scavenger burned and he fell at the feet of Black God. Spider then begged Black God to save his house and offered two prayersticks and two hoops if he would stop the fire. Black God accepted the offering and bade Water Sprinkler, his companion, put out the fire.

The eagles took their boy back to their home. Next day they again went hunting. Scavenger went for a walk and climbed a hill where he saw a coyote. He walked around the coyote which jumped up, touched the boy and turned him into a coyote. When the eagles returned at night they again looked for him but could not find him. The next morning they tracked him and at the end of the tracks found a scabby disreputable coyote. Since none but coyote tracks left the place, they decided the coyote must be their boy. They made a hoop and when they prayed, pushed the coyote through it. The skin cracked open at the top of his head. They shoved him through another hoop and the skin pulled back as far as his shoulders. When he was shoved through the third ring, the skin fell off to his hips and after passing through the fourth hoop, Scavenger stood restored. After the eagles had given him an emetic to cleanse him within, they took the boy home.

The next day the eagles once more left to hunt, and once more warned their boy not to leave the house. Disregarding the warning as usual, he wandered off and came to a place where a rock stood with two small rocks, one on top of the other. The black-tailed swallow had placed these rocks in this way to trap the Scavenger. He sat down on top of them and was buried under the rocks. When the eagles returned, they missed him and tracked him to the rocks, but they could find no tracks leaving that place.

They appealed for help to the Hunters of which Mountain Lion was chief. The Lion People decided the boy was under the rock. The Wolf, who belongs with the Hunting People, started to dig under the rock at the east side. He wore off his claws without accomplishing much. Lynx dug on the south side and did not make much progress. Bobcat dug at the west, and Badger at the north. Badger was the only one who made headway and he dug under the rock where he found only the bones of the Scavenger.

All working together, they took out the bones. They provided the skin from an unwounded deer, spread it out and laid the bones on it. They laid two feathers on each side of the skeleton and another perfect buckskin on top. They then called upon the Black, Blue, Yellow and White Medicine People who performed a ceremony. One of the four feathers belonged to Bald-headed Eagle and it became a wolf. The second feather belonging to Yellow Hawk became a mountain lion. When this transformation occurred, Scavenger came to life. The third feather belonging to Blue Hawk turned into a beaver; and the fourth, a magpie feather, became an otter. The skins of all these animals are now used in the Bead ceremony.

The day after all this had happened the eagles failed in a raid on their enemies, the Bee People, a group which included all the stinging insects. The eagles had told Scavenger to stay at home, but he followed and arrived after the retreat of the eagles. He killed all of the bees save two young ones. He gathered up the feathers of all the birds which had been killed in the raid and took them back to their home. He also took the hive and young bees back to the skyhole through which he dropped them to the earth. Up to this time there had been no bees on earth.

The next day the eagles, once more leaving their boy behind, went on a raid to the south where they met the Tumbleweed People. The wind blew the tumbleweed against them so hard that it killed all the eagles it hit, and the others had to retreat. Scavenger had followed again. He gathered some seed of the tumbleweed, then set the weeds afire and destroyed them. He dropped the seed to the earth through the skyhole, thus originating tumbleweed on the earth. He then restored the eagles which had been killed.

The eagles next went to attack the Rock People, and once more were overcome. Scavenger followed them and pounded the rocks into small pieces. He took small amounts of three kinds: red, yellow and white, and threw them through the skyhole, thus originating the minerals used in making sandpaintings. Once more he restored his friends.

The eagles made another raid, this time upon the Grass People. As usual, they were repulsed, but Scavenger followed, took some of the grass seed, piled up the grass and set fire to it. He threw the seed down to earth, restored the eagles which had been killed, and returned to the eagles' house.

The eagles were grateful for all the help Scavenger had rendered, and offered their choicest gift in return. They proposed that he marry one of their young girls and settle down to live with them. The wind whispered to him, "Don't do that! If you do, you will never see your mother, father, sister or brother again. Say that before you marry you would like to return to earth once more."

Scavenger took the wind's advice and the eagles taught him all the songs and prayers and gave him all the prayersticks and paraphernalia of the Bead Chant. The eagles dressed him in feathers and wings and by using them he was able to return to earth. He landed on top of Mt. Taylor, where he left the garments which enabled him to descend. Then he returned to his home which was at the foot of Whirling Mountain.

The Scavenger's mother, father, brother and sister had been mourning him ever since he disappeared. Now they were very glad to see him. Soon after his return he heard that the six Pueblo chiefs of the White House and six chiefs of the Blue House had been suffering greatly ever since they had been infected with the sores that resulted from their attack on the eagle's nest. The Scavenger announced that he could help them. They were desperate and gave him a roll of buckskin and other valuables for which he performed the Bead Chant over them. Scavenger did this, not only to cure the pueblo leaders, but also to teach his brother the ways of making the sandpaintings and performing the ceremony. After he had given the curative ceremony at which the brother learned all the details, Scavenger held a nine-day performance to initiate his brother and with this the brother was endowed with the power of curing. This was the first time the sandpaintings of the Bead Chant were used. After this the brother was called "Bead Singer," or "Bead Chanter."

When he was satisfied that his brother was trained in the lore of the Bead Chant, Scavenger returned to the place where he had hidden his feather garments, donned them and returned to the sky to marry the eagle maiden.

Sometime later Bead Chanter was called to Big Bead Place to perform a Bead Chant with a Fire Dance.

Meanwhile at a place called Black Mountain, a ceremony called the Awl Chant, which is no longer sung was being given. When a Fire Dance is to be given it is customary for runners to go out on the fifth day of the ceremony and hunt men who know other chants. When the runners arrive at the place where these men are, they give them ceremonial food and sprinkle them with corn meal. This rite constitutes an invitation for those visited to attend the Fire Dance with a dance troupe. The runner for the people from Black Mountain was Wolf, that from the Bead Chant was Mountain Lion. They met halfway between the two places at a place called "Water-in-amongst-the-white-sands." One said, "I was just going to your place." The other said, "I was just going to yours."

Each proposed that the other postpone his sing for one night, and they bargained back and forth. Wolf said to Mountain Lion, "If you would accept my proposal to put off your dance for one night, we should all be able to take in both ceremonies."

"That is a good idea," said Mountain Lion, "but the people wouldn't believe us."

Then Wolf said, "Let us exchange quivers to bind the agreement. We will keep our own bows." They agreed to this and exchanged, besides the quivers, the little parcels of food which they had with them.

PLATE V. *The Exchange of Quivers:* The four figures in this picture represent hunting animals. The white figure is Wolf. He carries a yellow quiver of mountain lion skin, belonging to the yellow Mountain Lion who faces him, Mountain Lion in turn carrying Wolf's white quiver made of wolf skin. Wolf's companion, Spotted Lion, carries a blue quiver made of lynx, and Spotted Lion, the companion of Mountain Lion, has a brown quiver made of wolverine (?) skin. All the quivers are slung over the shoulders by means of a rain streamer. Wolf's party had white bows, which they retain; Mountain Lion and his companion, Spotted Lion, carry dark bows.

The heads of the hunters, placed as is usual without regard for perspective, give the pictures a humorous effect. Each animal has a life (breath) feather: Wolf one of the yellow-tailed hawk, the others, one from white-tailed eagle. The four small lines up from the mouth in contrasting colors are whiskers. The headdresses of all the Hunters as well as that of the Rainbow are the bundles which were described for Plate I. The Rainbow carries only the reed wands in her hands. They are the same as those described for Plate I.

PLATE VI. *The Exchange of Quivers:* It is customary for the Navajo to use simpler or more complicated versions of the same picture. This is a more elaborate form of Plate V. Only the two leaders, Wolf and Mountain Lion, facing at the center, carry weapons. In addition they, as well as all the other figures, carry wands in their hands.

Each of the leaders, Wolf and Mountain Lion, has a party composed of a black Spotted Lion (Mexican jaguar), yellow Bobcat, blue Lynx and variegated Badger. Each has a different breath feather.

Bead Chanter was performing the ceremony for the Spider People who were the wealthiest of the Pueblos. The chief's daughter was kept hidden so that not even the sun could see her to shine on her. She wore a red feather bonnet of great value. The Spider People owned strings of turquoise as long as an arm and many beautiful beads of all kinds. Since Bead Chanter had never paid his brother for teaching him the Bead Chant, he planned to get the treasures of the Spider People to cancel his debt.

The wind told Scavenger that his brother was giving the ceremony. He decided to participate and returned to earth at Mt. Taylor, as he had done before. He wrapped his feather garments in a roll and carried them with him. The first night he spent at a place where a wolf had killed a deer and was eating it. The wolf ran away and Scavenger used the deer for food. He spent a second and third night on the way, expecting to arrive just in time for the last day of the ceremony. But, since Mountain Lion had agreed for the Spider People to postpone it one day, Scavenger arrived a day early.

That morning Bead Chanter had gone over to take part in the ceremony at Black Mountain. He dressed two of his men in eagle costumes to represent him and the Bead Chant in the Corral Dance. There he exchanged his rattle with the singer of the Awl Chant who gave him two prayer-sticks for it. For this reason no rattle is used in the Bead Chant. Immediately after dancing their dance at Black Mountain, when it was still dark, the troupe hastened back to Big Bead Place where Scavenger had arrived before his brother.

The people did not recognize the hero. His brother knew him but pretended he was a stranger. They had a secret conference at which Bead Chanter explained his plans for getting the treasures of the Spider People.

Among the valuables were dancing beads, beads which were dressed in feathers. In the Corral Dance these beads danced like people to the east, south, west, north and in the center. The mother of the chief's daughter had substituted imitation beads for the dancing beads and an imitation bonnet for her real red bonnet. As they were rehearsing the dance in the daytime, the Scavenger caused the center beads to stand still, insisting that their failure to dance was due to the fact that they were imitations. Runners were sent to the mother of the girl and told to insist on having the genuine articles.

Bead Chanter, not wishing to be implicated, said nothing and still pretended his brother was a stranger. Scavenger, after obtaining the real beads and bonnet, succeeded in performing the ceremony. The troupe practised all day and received much applause.

In the evening the people set up a huge corral after sprinkling sacred meal on the ground where the circle of hewn branches was to stand. When it was finished crowds of people moved in and the great fire was built in the center. The chanter from Black Mountain had brought his company to take part in the dance. The Wolf People joined in a dance with the Lion People, all carrying packs of corn on their backs.

They had secured the corn by using their powers which enabled them to plant, cultivate and harvest it in a few minutes, this magic being one of the tricks they performed before their dance. Singers from all the chants—Night, Shooting, Water, and all the others—were represented in a dance fitting to each. The dances continued around the great fire until dawn.

PLATE VII. *The Hunting Animals with Cornpacks:* This picture represents the Hunters at their dance on the last night when the Bead Chant was represented at the Corral or Fire Dance. In Plates

V and VI the agreement for them to attend is represented. They now have put aside their weapons and hold the sacred wands in their hands.

The triangular pieces on their backs represent packs of corn which was grown in miraculous fashion, as the corn-growing event of the Corral Dance.

During this time Wind had gone back to the sky to inform the Eagle People of what was happening on earth. When the time came, near dawn, for the rite of the dancing beads, they lowered a cloud near the earth, but they could not find the Scavenger. At last they found him asleep in the corral. They wakened him and asked him to eat, but he refused because he knew that if he did the lightning would not be able to raise him. The Scavenger now took the occasion to whisper to his brother, saying they would never meet on earth again, but that he would be with his brother to help him spiritually. He told the Chanter never to give a Fire (Corral) Dance with the Bead Chant again.

Then the Scavenger put on his eagle garments which up to this time he had kept hidden. Bead Chanter began to drum on the inverted basket and his wonderful brother danced with the dancing beads to the east, south, west and north. As he danced toward the center he began to rise, taking with him the treasures of the Spider People. Two streaks of lightning came down and lifted him to the clouds and the eagles hidden there bore him the rest of the way to the sky.

PLATE VIII. *The Final Ascension of Scavenger Attended by Eagles:* There are two paintings of the final ascension of Scavenger, each stressing, as is so often the case, a different phase of the same scene. In this plate the boy is shown with a bird body and wings of all the eagles and hawks which aided him. He has the yellow whistle on his breast, and above it, the crystal; the whistle to furnish air, the crystal to give him light in the darkness of the cloud in which he was enveloped.

The birds at each side are the same as those of Plate III: bald-headed eagles, yellow-tailed hawks, big blue hawks, big white hawks, big black hawks, black and white eagles. They carry zig-zag lightnings or rainbows in their feet to represent the ropes with which Scavenger was conveyed.

The guardian which surrounds all sides of the picture except the east is in this case composed of feathers which may be real feathers from the chanter's bundle, or may be strewn in sand.

PLATE IX. *The Final Ascension of Scavenger Attended by Lightnings (Snakes):* The figure of the Scavenger is like the one of Plate VIII except: there is no lightning between his feet; the wings given him by the white eagles are here shown in pink; beads of all colors decorate his body, showing his triumph over the Spider People who previously owned them; a lightning and rain streamer connect him with one bald-headed eagle and one black-white eagle who stand for all the eagles and hawks who helped the boy.

Lightnings and snakes are identical, or at least interchangeable, in Navajo thought. The Black and Blue Snakes with lightning on their bodies and feathers at their joints stand for the lightnings which lifted the boy from the earth to the cloud they had waiting for him, and thence the birds were able to carry him.

Two bats guard the entrance. Bat is a savior in many Navajo myths, but no mention of her (she is often an old woman) is made in this legend.

The Spider People, shouting with rage, brought out their bows and arrows. Bead Chanter quieted them saying it was their own fault since they had allowed a stranger to dance with their valuables. Thus Bead Chanter repaid his brother for transmitting his learning and power, and at the same time avenged the wrongs done to his brother.

After Scavenger had reached the sky he became worried about his brother. He told the wind to go back to find out what had happened. He told the wind to tell the Bead Chanter never to include the Fire Dance in the Bead Chant again. He sent certain plants which his brother did not have. Then he sent the news that the people in the sky had quarreled over the treasures he had brought back, and finally all had received some share of them. To the sun a long string of turquoise had been given, as well as the red feather bonnet. The reflection of the bonnet may now be seen in the afterglow of the sunset.

Because of all these happenings the Bead Chant now has no Fire Dance, corn is no longer grown magically in the Fire Dance, nor is there the dance of the dancing beads. There is no rattle in the Bead Chant. There is a taboo against people going to sleep in the dance corral.

V

Legends and Sandpaintings of the Male Shooting Chant:
The Visit to the Sun

IN 1924 A MYTH recounting the adventures of the Holy Twins insofar as they had to do with the origin of the Male Shooting Chant According-to-holiness was recorded in Navajo from dictation by Gray Eyes of Lukachukai, from whom Miguelito learned the Shooting Chant. Two brief summaries[1] have been published in English, each little more than an abstract of the original myth which is very long. A long narrative accompanies the Huckel paintings which seems to have been related primarily from the point of view of connecting the large number of sandpaintings belonging to the collection.

Since this myth differs in a number of details from the one already published, since it includes the paintings and story of the evil-chasing phase as well as the one called according-to-holiness and those of the Fire Dance form of the chant; and above all, because it is exceptionally clear and well-organized, it has been deemed appropriate to use the legend here with all the details given by Miguelito.

Gray Eyes dwelt at length upon conditions on the earth before the birth of the Twins and their struggles in overcoming the monsters. It may be, as other chanters have averred, that these adventures are part of the basic knowledge which all medicine men must possess—a part, I should venture, of the Blessing Chant—which Gray Eyes included in the introduction of his legend. Chanters differ greatly in the emphasis they lay upon one detail or another. Many consider their lore the more authentic the farther back into mythological times it goes. Some, like Gray Eyes and Miguelito, take pride in stressing the plot and the relationship of the chant details to plot; others, as in other versions I have recorded, have a punctilious interest in the ceremonial details and very little in the plot. To them the legend serves to explain what they have been taught to do, but they do not dwell upon the mythical drama.

The legend Miguelito told is in almost all respects supplementary and complementary to that of Gray Eyes. In details, and not in essentials, does it differ. I believe the reason for this is that it stresses the evil-chasing side, although there can be no doubt that it includes also the chant according-to-holiness. I have already (p. 2) noted the difficulties Miguelito must have had in giving this story to Mr. Schweizer. Not the least of them was to reconcile the Fire Dance version with the evil-chasing, since these two are never given together. However the necessity faced by the old chanter on this occasion has made it possible for us to understand many points of organization and relationship which would otherwise remain obscure.

The myth, which will be related together with descriptions of the paintings, in the order in which they were learned by the Holy Ones, is a masterly unit. It includes not only explanations of all the paintings in the Huckel Collections, but also of many in the Bush Collection at Columbia University. Since many paintings from the latter have been published[2] they will not be repeated,

---

[1] Newcomb, Franc J. and Reichard, Gladys A. *Sandpaintings of the Navajo Shooting Chant*, pp. 24-41.
  Reichard, Gladys A. *Spider Woman*, pp. 169-179.
[2] Newcomb-Reichard, *loc. cit.*

but references to them will be made to show how they fit into the chant. The myth follows with descriptions of the paintings where they belong:

Changing Woman was living at the Place-of-emergence[1] where Holy Man, Holy Boy, Holy Woman and Holy Girl were born. Holy Woman and Holy Girl were born for the purpose of giving the people the Female Shooting Chant and later the Water and Hail Chants. They went to live with Arrow and Locust People (who are the same) and lived nearby.

Holy Man and Holy Boy were born for the purpose of originating the Male chants.

Big Monster, who lived at a place called Hot Water, destroyed Earth People as fast as they were created and made the world unfit for habitation by human beings.

Changing Woman succeeded in keeping Holy Man and Holy Boy hidden until they were twelve days old. These wonderful children attained in a day what ordinary children lived a year to accomplish. For four days she kept them wrapped in a dark cloud in which she had placed a turquoise dish containing corn, real pollen (*i.e.*, the pollen of wide reed), blue pollen (the petals of larkspur), pollen of buffalo grass and other strong foods. Strong foods are those which give a child supernatural powers at the same time that they make him grow rapidly. The fourth day the children could walk and their mother made them a ball to play with. This took up their time and interest for four days more. She then made them bows and arrows with which they played for three days.

On the twelfth night they asked who their father was and their mother refused to tell them. Exactly at dawn of the twelfth day the boys ran a long race to the east. When they returned, they threatened to kill their mother with arrows if she did not tell them who their father was. She answered that she was very sorry, but their father lived so far away and the way was so thickly beset with dangers of all kinds that it would be impossible for them to go to him. For this reason it was useless for her to tell who he was or where he lived. They begged her three times and she refused to tell. The fourth time she thought it would be easier to tell who he was than where he lived and she said, "The Sun is your father."

They ate their breakfast of unflavored gruel, *i.e.*, gruel without cedar ashes, then went outside and said, "Let's go to our father," and at once started off.

They first came to a place called Hill-of-many-points, meaning it was made of material like chipped agate. There a little bird, the cedar waxwing, lived. "Where are you going, my grandchildren?" he inquired. "To the home of our father, the Sun," they answered.

"Gracious! there are many obstacles in your way. You have come to me for help but all I can do for you is to give you this string of flint knives." So saying he hung a string of flint points around each of their necks.

The boys went on and came to a place called Lake-of-heavy-wood, where they found another small bird. "Where are you going, my grandchildren?" he asked. "To the house of our father, the Sun."

"You will have a hard time. You will have many hardships and suffer greatly. I wish I could help you but I cannot do more than give you two songs," and he gave them the songs.

They went on to a place called Wide Valley, where they met a worm like a large caterpillar, of changeable color, with only one horn. He said, "Where are you going? Earth People never come here." "To the house of our father, the Sun." "Oh! then you are my grandchildren. You will find twelve guards at the house of the Sun: four bears, four snakes and four thunders."

He told them the names of the guardians so that the boys would have power over them. Then he told them that the Sun would test them in various ways. One trial was to try to kill them with

<hr/>

[1] The Navajo, like most of the Southwest Indians, believe that they emerged from various worlds under the present world. The Place-of-emergence is therefore of great importance ceremonially, and it is usually represented as dark, since it is believed that the struggle of the Navajo to come out to this world was a struggle out of darkness.

tobacco. In order to help them pass the tobacco test he exuded a brown fluid which they were to use as an antidote to the Sun's poison. He gave them also two feathers of eagle down.

They went on and came to a swamp where Cutting Reeds grew. They looked nice, but Wind warned the boys that the leaves would cut them to pieces, but that the down feathers would take them up to the sky. The boys mounted their feathers and were carried up through the skyhole.

They could see the house of the Sun above the horizon. At the top was a white streak, under it a black stripe, then a blue, and at the bottom, a yellow band. The bears on guard growled, but as soon as their names were mentioned they quieted down.

The snake guardians hissed at them, but as soon as the boys mentioned their names, one by one, the snakes let them pass. They came to Black Thunder who thundered at them. "You, our grandfather, raised as we were, in the black cloud, we are your grandchildren. Let us pass." At once they passed. They encountered Blue, Yellow and Variegated (Pink) Thunder who let the boys pass through after their names had been uttered.

They came then into the house of the Sun where a woman who resembled their own mother sat. She was silent for some time, then said, "Earth People never come here." "Answer quickly!" prompted the Wind. "We came in search of our father. People told us he lives here."

The woman looked surprised and said, "He is out now, but he will soon be back. What do you want to eat, my children?" "Nothing," they replied. Then she told them that their father was fearsome, and she hid them in the cloud of mixed colors at the north side of the house. There was a curtain of black at the east, one of blue at the west, and one of yellow at the south.

In the evening the Sun returned, coming into the house and asking boisterously, "Where are the visitors?" The first three times he asked, his wife answered she had not seen any. When he asked for the fourth time, she burst forth in a jealous rage, "Two boys came here claiming you are their father!"

Sun looked around and, not seeing anyone, pulled down the black cloud at the east and found nothing. He did the same with the blue cloud of the west, the yellow cloud of the south and found nothing. Finally, pulling down the pink cloud curtain of the north, he found the two boys.

Using no term of address, he said gruffly, "Where do you come from? Earth People do not come here."

Then he asked them if they had any tobacco and they said they had none. Whereupon he drew out his tobacco and prepared a smoke for them in a turquoise pipe, lighting it with his own heat. They remembered the warning given them by the horned worm, and when the Sun was not looking, took the antidote out of their ears and put it into their mouths.

Holy Man smoked first and returned the pipe to the Sun who said doubtfully, "Perhaps so." He refilled it and gave it to Holy Boy who took a long pull and handed it back. "Perhaps you *are* my children," said Sun reluctantly.

Then he asked them if they wanted to eat and they refused food. "Well, night has come on and you had better stay, but there is no place inside for you to sleep." He took them outside and left them on a rock, which immediately became surrounded by water. Then he secretly called Cold to freeze them to death, and returned to his house. Otter came up out of the water and kept them warm, but when he returned to the water at daylight he warned them not to tell anyone.

During the night Holy Man dreamed that they were back on earth and that the rock had grown up through the skyhole with them. After Otter left he told his brother about his dream. Then Sun came out to look for them, expecting to find them dead. He found them very lively but covered with frost because of the perspiration caused by Otter's warmth. "Get up! What do you mean by sleeping so late!" he scolded. When they rose, he said, "Perhaps you are my children."

He took them into the house again and there they saw the Moon. Sun said to him, "My uncle, go build a fire in the sweathouse for your grandchildren." The Moon built a fire in the sweathouse and then dug a deep hole at the back of it. He covered it with a large slab of white stone; on that he placed another of blue stone, then one of variegated stone and, on top, a black one. He then brought in stones for the fire. He told the boys about the hole at the back before he started the fire.

Sun took the children to the sweathouse and closed it in tight. The fire had been started and the stones were beginning to get hot. Sun returned and called in, "Are you warm?" "No," they answered. Three times they answered "No" to his question, but the fourth time they said "Yes."

They had climbed into the hole each time, displacing one of the slabs of precious stone which Moon had put into it. Each time the Sun had spoken to them, he had poured water on the hot stones, expecting to scald them to death with steam.

The heat melted the black stone, and it became jet (cannel coal). When the heat hit the variegated stone it made red streaks and it became abalone. The blue stone became turquoise and the white stone became whiteshell streaked with yellow because of the heat.

When the steam had evaporated and the stones had cooled, the boys came out of the hole and sat quietly in the sweathouse. When the Sun saw them sitting there unharmed he remarked, "Perhaps you are my children." Three times he had failed to kill them.

The Sun now took them back to the house. There were four pillars in the house. Each one was hollow and fitted with inverted obsidian points which moved up and down in a grinding fashion. The pillar at the east was black, that at the south, blue; the one at the west, yellow; and the north one was white. The Sun put the boys into the black grinder at the east, expecting them to be ground to pieces. The boys wrapped themselves in the eagle-down feathers given them by the horned worm and escaped this trial unharmed. They were placed successively in the blue, yellow and white grinders and emerged safely each time. Four times the Sun had tested them and the boys survived uninjured.

While Holy Man and Holy Boy had been undergoing these trials, Changing Woman at her home was praying for their safe return and, appealing to Enemy Slayer for help, she had made offerings and paintings.

PLATE X. *Holy Man Guarded by Monster Slayer and Child-of-the-water:* This painting illustrates the Holy Twins in their guise as War gods fully armed, and in the form which they assumed as Earth People. It is difficult for us to imagine two individuals guarding themselves, yet that is exactly what this picture represents. In the mythological or miracle world and times, the Navajo gods could be multiplied so that one could be here, another exactly like it—or better another "self" of that same being—somewhere else. So it happens that the Sacred Twins, Monster Slayer the figure in black, and Child-of-the-water, the blue figure, are guarding Holy Man (who is the same as his mate, Holy Boy), a representative of themselves in a different rôle (see p. 15).

Holy Man (and Holy Boy as well) is depicted as a black figure decorated with white zigzag lightnings. These protect his feet, legs, body and arms. In his rôle as more nearly human, the lightnings at the feet are female, that is simply crossed at the ends, instead of male with barbed points as they are in the other two figures. The necks of all figures in the sandpaintings are blue, signifying things pertaining to the earth, and each has four red marks indicating the breath of life.

Faces of "people" in the Shooting Chant are brown. The streak of yellow (pollen) at the chin represents evening light and the streak of white (cornmeal) on the forehead stands for dawn. The black line above the forehead indicates hair; the red one, hair from elk or antelope, a ceremonial requirement. The blue and red ornaments on the breast are turquoise and redstone necklaces, and the strings hanging from the ears are of the same materials. On his head Holy Man (and his two "self-protectors") wears the head bundle of the Shooting Chant which represents a waterspout similar to those of the wings of the Thunders (see p. 60). The white feather is an eagle-down feather which gives lightness and speed. The small blue circle represents the chant token, a small but perfect turquoise bead tied with an olivella shell, which a person for whom the chant has been sung wears at all times to show he is protected by arrows, snakes and lightning.

Holy Man holds the eagle-feathered arrow in his right hand, and in his left, the black bow, both of which were given him by his father, the Sun.

The figures of the War gods have many features in common. They are fully armed in flint from toe to head. Zigzag (male) lightnings shoot out from the feet, hands, head and club of Monster Slayer, the black figure, and lightnings protect his head. The odd-shaped object in his right hand is his club made of flint and reinforced by the lightning which darts in every direction. The red feather above the head bundle signifies the redstone arrow given by the Sun, consequently speed and power.

The differences between Monster Slayer and his brother are slight. Blue flint armor protects him; it is reinforced by straight lightning at feet, hands, head and club. The blue head feather represents the turquoise arrow of the Sun.

All three figures are given skirts with elaborate patterns as was Scavenger of the Bead Chant. Above the skirts at the right side of each one hangs a pouch. Some figures are given a belt or sash, others, one of these ornate pouches. They represent a treasured article of trade which the Navajo used to get from the Plains Indians. The pouch was made of buckskin—in early days, embroidered with porcupine quillwork; after the coming of the white man, with beads.

The entire picture is protected by black and white lightning, the black points barbed to indicate maleness, the white ones smooth for femaleness.

A companion picture shows Holy Woman protected by Monster Slayer and Child-of-the-water. She is depicted like the middle figure of Plate XX and the lightning guardian around the whole has the colors black and white reversed, white being outside.

The picture of Holy Man is used if the patient is a man; the one of Holy Woman, if the patient is a woman.

The Sun finally called them "My children!" But he said, "My children, there is something else I want you to do."

Sun had two boys and two girls by the wife who lived with him in the sky. The boys were outside. The Sun had the girls sit at one side of the house and placed near them four images. Then he said, "Each of you choose a girl to bless the images. They are also my children. Which one will you have for your sister?" Four times Sun repeated this question. Wind whispered to Holy Man to take the one next to the end at the right. He pointed at that one and a girl stepped down. Wind whispered to Holy Boy to take the one next to the end at the left, and a girl stepped down. Sun ordered the girls to go out and get soapweed with which to wash the hair of their brothers and once more addressed the boys as his children.

When the girls came back they had soapweed and two baskets, one of turquoise and one of whiteshell. Each girl washed the hair of the boy who had chosen her and blessed him and dried him with cornmeal.

The boys' hair had been short and tousled. When the girls rubbed their hands over the top of the heads and down the backs, the hair became long and smooth. The limbs of the youths were rough and scrawny, and when the girls rubbed them with blessing, their arms and legs became strong and clean.

The bows and arrows which Changing Woman had given the boys were made of cedar (juniper). The Sun took these away and gave each of them a large black bow. To Holy Man he gave an eagle-feathered arrow and to Holy Boy the arrow which has white and yellow feathers.

Now he asked his newly acknowledged sons what they subsisted on, for they had not eaten since they arrived at the Sun's house. "Pollen," they answered. The girls placed before them pollen in an abalone basket. And though there was only a bit of pollen in each basket, there remained always the same amount no matter how much the boys ate.

After they finished eating, the woman also acknowledged them, "You are my children as well. Your two brothers who were outside playing have been bitten by a watersnake. I have heard that Earth People know many cures. Can you cure your brothers of snakebite?'' They answered, ''We have no medicine with us.'' But just then Wind brought some plants from the earth and whispered how to use them for curing. Holy Man and Holy Boy pressed the herbs to their lips, then gave them to the boys to chew and at once they were well. The Sun told Holy Man that he should never try to depict watersnake in the sandpaintings because it had bitten the Sun's son.

The mother was much pleased and turned to the Sun saying, ''Why do you not stay home part of the time? Your children have come a long way to see you and you ought to spend at least a day with them.''

The Sun, who was really the bearer of the light-giving, heat-giving sun, agreed to the proposal and sent the Wind out to carry the sun that day, so he could spend the day with his newly found children.

The Sun took this time to instruct his earthborn children in the arts of healing, of which making sandpaintings was a great part. The first paintings he showed them were those of the Skies with domesticated Plants, the Skies without Plants, and the Sun's House itself.

FIGURE 1. *The Sun's House:* The painting represents a boothlike arrangement called the Sun's House which is a part of the chanter's bundle. A chanter may, however, not own such a property; in which case he may depict the Sun's House in a painting like this one. The foundation consists of four wide stripes: yellow, at the bottom, representing evening light; blue next, representing blue sky; then black for night; and at the top, white for dawn.

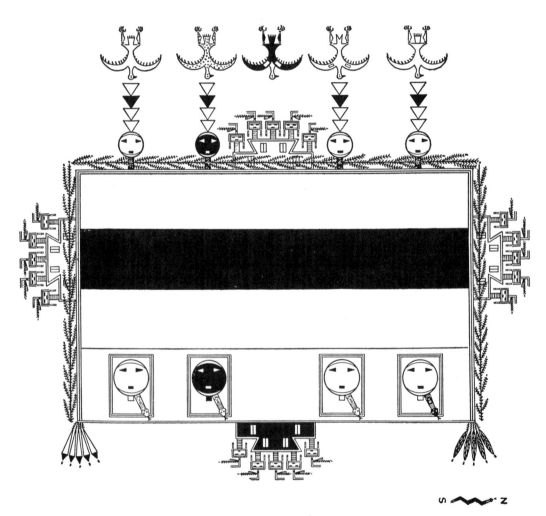

FIGURE I. THE SUN'S HOUSE

On the bottom band of yellow the circular figures from left to right represent: Yellow Wind, Black Wind, Moon (white), Sun (blue), each at one of the entrances to the Sun's House, surrounded by a rainbow and guarded by a snake of contrasting color. Corresponding circular figures are placed immediately above the structure and represent the same powers. Above them rise cloud symbols shown in superimposed triangles of the same colors as the booth itself: yellow at the bottom, next blue, then black and white.

Above are five birds which, in the more realistic setup, are hung from the *hogan* ceiling on strings or wires, pulled during the ceremony by an assistant in hiding behind the booth. This helper also blows whistles to imitate the sound of the birds as they fly about.

A rainbow garland bounds the entire structure of the Sun's House and thick boughs of Douglas fir and Colorado blue spruce are banked over and around it. The branchlike lines of the picture represent these.

At the four sides of the Sun's House are symbols of the skyhole in the different colors: black at the east, yellow at the south, blue at the west and pink at the north. The little faces which peer out over them represent Sky People of various kinds: black Sky People, living near the black entrance to the sky; Sun People, living near the yellow entrance; Water People, whose home is represented by blue; and Summer People, represented in a pink or glistening home. (Newcomb-

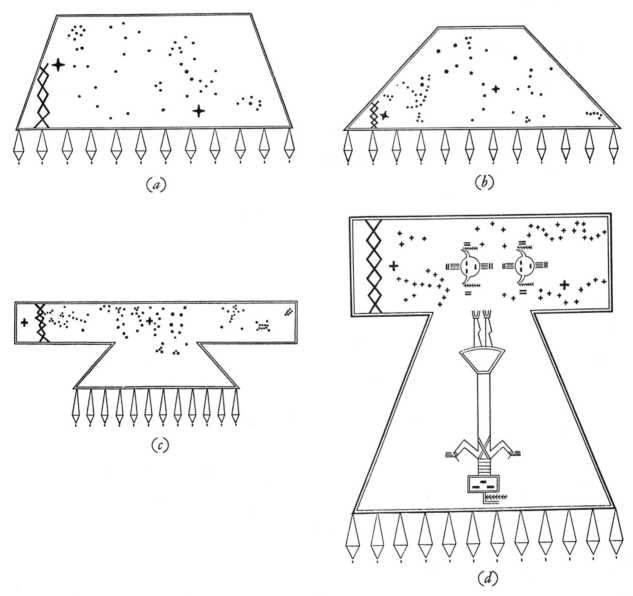

FIGURE 2. REPRESENTATIONS OF THE NIGHT SKY

Reichard, Plate XIX, is a variant of this picture. In that work there are errors of title and explanation; they should be as given here).

The other two paintings given by the Sun to his children at this time have many variants. Although the themes remain the same, they are carried out with greater or smaller differences. Miguelito emphasizes the importance of these paintings and it is borne out by the frequent use of one or the other in almost every performance of the Shooting Chant.

The center of the Sky paintings depicts Sun, Moon, Black and Yellow Winds. The simplest form is shown in Newcomb-Reichard, Figure 8. In addition to the center motives, there may be representations of Dawn, Blue Sky, Evening Light and Night Sky. A painting in the Huckel Collections is practically identical with that of Newcomb-Reichard Figure 9. In these the domesticated plants, corn, bean, squash and tobacco fill the corners. Rainbow connects the Blue Sky, Evening Light and Night Sky, and Sun Pouch and Bat guard the eastern opening. This picture was used on the wall at the right of the fireplace in the lobby of El Navajo Hotel at Gallup.

Still another variant lacks the domesticated plants, but each "sky," represented by a rectangular symbol, has a "tail," "wing," or "feather," which indicates the flight of time, or more specifically, the departure of Holy Man from his father's home on the wings of the morning. Newcomb-Reichard, Plate XVIII, varies further from this in that the "wing" is enlarged and on it a personage of the "sky" is Dawn Boy.

Since these pictures are among the best known, they are not reproduced here, but Figure 2 illustrates differences in the Night Sky, since the stars are represented differently according to the time of year when the picture is made. Figure 2, *a* was painted in the summer, Figure 2, *b* in March. Figure 2, *c* was also painted in the summer, but either earlier or later than Figure 2, *d* so that the large star is west instead of east of the Milky Way, which is represented by connected diamond designs. Other slight differences are also apparent. The stars of Newcomb-Reichard (Figure 2, *d* here) correspond more closely to Figure 2, *b* but are not identical. Of the eight versions of these pictures which we have, no two are exactly alike, but we do not know just when each was painted.

After he had taught them the three paintings, the Sun took the boys to the top of the high rock and showed them the whole universe, pointing out every important spot, and drilling them on the names of the places he mentioned.

He next showed them the four jewel arrows of turquoise, whiteshell, abalone and redstone. He told them that if anything should happen to these arrows nothing could be done to replace them and for this reason he could not give them up. But to represent them, he gave the eagle-feathered arrow, the feathered wand, the yellow tail-feathered arrow, and the red-feathered wand. All these were to be used in the Chant when it was sung "according-to-holiness." The Sun then gave them a "talking prayerstick" which was to be used when the chant was sung for "evil-chasing."

He taught his children the uses of lightning and rainbow symbols. Then he showed them black herbs at the east, blue herbs at the west, yellow at the south, and mixed-colored herbs at the north. He told them they would find all of these herbs on the earth at the place where they came out of the darkness.

Next he gave them two more paintings, the painting of the Earth and Sky, and the Emergence of the Medicine People.

FIGURE 3. *The Emergence of the Medicine People:* The Navajo think of herbs as "medicines," that is, as plants with healing powers, and that is the reason the term is used here. Plants may be considered animate and possessing all the powers and characteristics of man, hence, they are "people."

It is believed that the "medicines" emerged from darkness, the center of the picture, even as the human Navajo did. The heads of twelve of them may be seen on each side of the dark central square which represents the place of emergence—black plants at the east, blue at the south, white at the west, and pink (or glistening) at the north.

Holy Man, standing on a rainbow at the east, shows his acceptance of the gift of the black herbs by holding five in each hand; Holy Boy, at the south, holds five blue plants in each hand.

At the west is Holy Woman with five white herbs in each hand; and Holy Girl stands at the north holding pink herbs. Plants of colors corresponding to those of the center grow from each corner of the black center.

A Rainbow person guards three sides of the picture, and Sun's Tobacco Pouch and Big Fly are the eastern guards.

The painting of the Earth and Sky is basic and may be used in a large number of chants, perhaps in all or at least most of them. It is drawn in Newcomb-Reichard, Figure 5.

"The yellow of the sky (male) represents the evening light, the hands, the white dawn.

"A legend not belonging to the Shooting Chant tells of a time when the male sky and female earth had a quarrel and asked for a separation. The sky agreed saying, 'I will send no more rain to you.'

"As a result there was a great drought on earth. The streams dried up and all the vegetation was dying. Then Mother Earth asked for a reconciliation which was made. The rains fell once more and the plants grew and furnished food. This picture shows the reconciliation between Sky Father and Earth Mother." This picture is painted at the left of the fireplace in the lobby of El Navajo Hotel.

The Sun then explained the rattles to his sons. He told their names and showed how they were made. He said these rattles were really big snakes. He gave them a black rattle calling it "Big

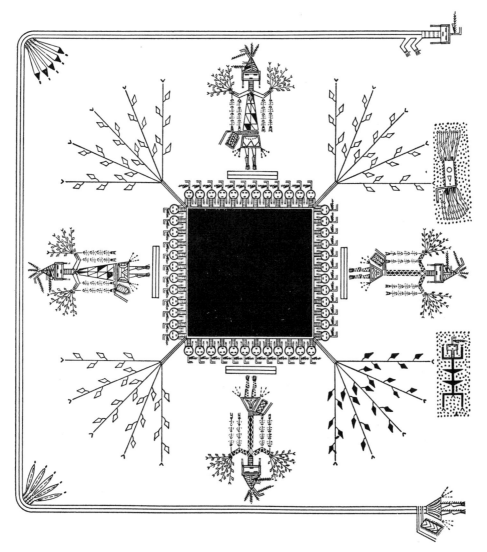

FIGURE 3. THE EMERGENCE OF THE MEDICINE PEOPLE

Dark Snake" rattle. Then he gave them a blue rattle which he said was very important because it represented the Sun himself and stood for light and divinity, names he used also to indicate his two sons.

After teaching them the many details concerned with all this chant lore, Sun took Holy Man on the turquoise arrow and Holy Boy on the whiteshell arrow to the skyhole. When they arrived there the Sun told them to point out the place on earth whence they had come. The Wind whispered to them where to point. The Sun then pointed out the four sacred mountains, and also the Place-of-emergence where the people came out of darkness. He told them that there they would find all the things he had mentioned when he had instructed them. "There it is," he said, "that the Arrow and Locust People live. Their chief knows everything as well as I do and he will teach you. There too grow all the herbs necessary to the chant."

Just before he left them the Sun said he would give them one more test of their power. They should try to take down the sun at noon of the following day. Then he left them; and the blue and white arrows carried them down to earth, and moisture fell with their descent. At the place where they landed they found four tracks made by Changing Woman to guide them into her *hogan*. The two tracks for the right foot were made of white cornmeal; the two for the left foot, of pollen. When the boys entered the house they found a large gathering of people. They spent the night telling of their experiences.

The next morning Holy Man went outside, but heard no sign, so went back in. Then Holy Boy went out and heard Big Fly coming from the sky. Big Fly lit on his shoulder and whispered that he should try to take the sun down before noon, because if he waited until later, it would be impossible to do so. He also said that there were two paintings the Sun had not described. One was of the Whirling Feathers which would help them in lowering the Sun. Big Fly told them how to make it, and also how to take down the sun by holding the sacred arrows in their hands. The other was of the Sun in Eclipse, for which they would have use later.

Meanwhile the people in the *hogan* had been discussing the adventures of Holy Man and Holy Boy. Coyote was in the crowd and he said, "There is something missing. The story is not complete." Four times he said this, intimating that the story was all right so far but that it had no future. "The fellows have four arrows, but there are only two people to use them. Over at the house of the Arrow-locust People are two girls, Holy Woman and Holy Girl."

Holy Man and Holy Boy went over and got the girls. While they were gone the people started the painting of the Whirling Feathers. Even after the boys had brought back the two girls Coyote said, "There is still something missing." The people made the house in the center of the painting, and Holy Man, Holy Boy, Holy Woman and Holy Girl each stood at one of the four directions. Holy Man and Holy Boy reached up with their large black bows and pulled down the sun and moon. Holy Woman and Holy Girl each had yellow bows and pulled down black and yellow winds, respectively.

In Gray Eyes' legend of the Shooting Chant there is an interesting episode of Holy Man's encounter with Mr. Turtledove who had charge of the Whirling-tail-feather (Newcomb-Reichard, p. 34, Plate XXXIV); but no mention is made that the Twins were to use it in bringing down the Sun. With this function, as recounted by Miguelito, it forms a companion picture to that of Bringing-down-the-sun (Cp. Newcomb-Reichard Plate XIV), in which the Holy People are drawn in a line and each has a bow and a feathered basket in which Sun, Moon and Black and Yellow Winds are carried.

FIGURE 4. *The Whirling Feathers:* This picture of the Huckel Collections differs from the one just referred to in that the drawing of all parts is more detailed and delicate, and the colors are placed differently. Holy Man at the east is touching the basket in which the blue Sun rests with his bow. At the south, Holy Boy brings down the Black Wind; at the west, Holy Woman overcomes the white Moon; and at the north, Holy Girl shows her power over Yellow Wind. The feathers surrounding the central Moon figure correspond in color with the "sun" figure in each quarter.

The rainbow garland encircles the picture and white and black Big Flies guard the east.

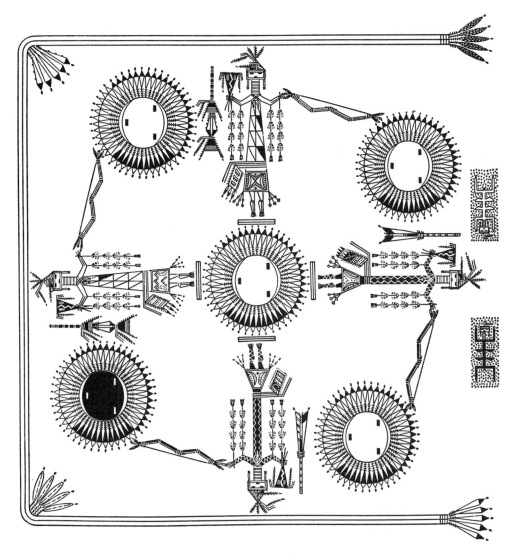

FIGURE 4. THE WHIRLING FEATHERS

Holy Man now threw the eagle-feathered arrow with the turquoise bead at the painting of the sun and told the figure to swallow the arrow. When the sun refused to do so, Holy Man swallowed it himself. Holy Woman did the same with the white-feathered wand, Holy Boy with the yellow tail-feathered arrow, and Holy Girl with the red-feathered wand. The people all screamed with horror when they did this. The Sun then spoke to his sons saying that they had proved their power and had done no harm. Then he told them to sprinkle sacred meal and to make the painting Taking Down the Sun.

FIGURE 5. *Taking Down the Sun:* This picture has many details in common with Figure 4. The Holy People are arranged in the same way and, in addition to the bow, arrow, and rattle which each carries, there is also a basket carried in the left hand. Each one of the Holy People had this in which to receive his "sun" after it had been brought down. Sun, Black Wind, Moon and Yellow Wind are shown at the end of the respective bows. They have horns to designate power, and lines representing rain extend to short rainbows on each side. This is the way the same powers are represented in the center of the pictures representing the "skies." The feathered designs of Figure 4, with the Sun and companions in the center, represent the baskets in which they are carried. In this picture the natural phenomena themselves are emphasized instead of these containers.

The bows of the two female Holy Ones are tilted in a different position from those of the males. That is because they slipped.

As usual, the center differs. Rainbows are inside, supposedly surrounding one of the homes of Changing Woman. The feathers parallel to them represent the feathers of the symbolic arrows used on earth, and next to them are the Sun's sacred arrows of precious stones.

The reference in the myth to the arrow-swallowing accounts for the trick of arrow-swallowing, which is one of the most awe-inspiring events of the Fire Dance performance.

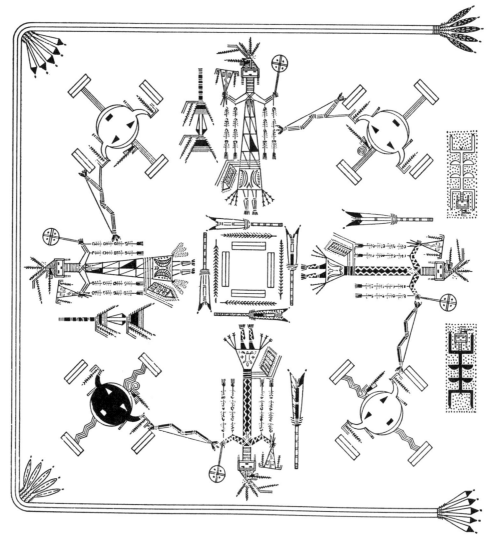

FIGURE 5. TAKING DOWN THE SUN

After all this was over, Sun told them to send Sun, Moon, Black and Yellow Winds back to their places. "Hereafter," he continued, "If anything happens to the sun or moon use the eclipse paintings," and he went on to show these paintings to the boys.

One of the eclipse paintings, the Eclipse of the Sun, is illustrated in Newcomb-Reichard, Plate XI (p. 56). The pair Sun and Moon in Eclipse are practically identical in this and the Huckel Collections. The painting of the Sun in Eclipse is used when the patient is a man; that of the Moon in

Eclipse for a woman patient. One of these is painted on the wall at the left of the fireplace in the lobby of El Navajo Hotel.

"The eclipse of the Sun or Moon indicates that Sun is displeased. It is a time when all normal activities, particularly ceremonial proceedings, should cease. The people must wait until the eclipse is over. If a child is born during an eclipse, a one-night ceremony must be performed for it as soon as it is old enough to speak, and at that time one of these paintings is made."

(It is interesting to note, in connection with world-wide legends explaining that the sun is swallowed during an eclipse, that the Navajo have no such notion. The two large snakes surrounding each figure, Sun or Moon, are not there because they had to do with the disappearance of the luminary, but because they are the guardians of the Sun's House.

On November 13, 1938 the painting of Sun in Eclipse was made for a Navajo baby about five months old. The date of his birthday was known exactly and had nothing to do with an eclipse. By questioning and interrelating known facts I discovered that the man who diagnosed the baby's case and recommended the ceremony he was to have had done so on November 7, 1938, when there was a total eclipse of the moon visible on the Navajo reservation. *Author's Note.*)

Now the Sun spoke seriously to his children, "My children, I have not asked you for anything, although I have taught you much."

They then set before their father baskets of turquoise, whiteshell, abalone and redstone. They placed the arrows and wands on the baskets in alternating directions. The people offered up prayers for rain, corn, tobacco and vegetation of all kinds and as they did so, they placed beads in the basket corresponding to the material it was made of. When they had finished the Sun returned to the sky carrying the precious baskets with their sacred contents.

At this time Changing Woman made a painting of corn as her offering to the Sun.

The painting here referred to is that of Newcomb-Reichard, Figure 10, Blue Corn People with Pollen Boy and Cornbug Girl. It is proper that a bird should light upon paintings of the Corn. The Blue Corn People of Figure 10 referred to do not have birds on their heads; those of the Huckel Collections have. From south to north the birds are: bluebird, blue swallow, oriole, canary.

"The blue corn personified symbolizes the life of the corn. The Pollen Boy represents germination; Cornbug Girl, reproduction."

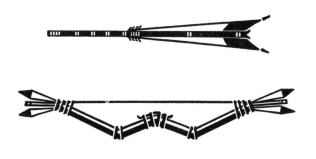

VI

Legend and Sandpaintings of the Male Shooting Chant: Adventures among Earth People

CHANGING WOMAN AND HER TWO SONS and two daughters now went back to the Place-of-emergence where they saw the paintings of the Arrow People and got instructions from their chief, as the Sun had advised them to do. The three arrow paintings were a part of this knowledge.

The chief of the Arrow People had a sacred black grebe which had a white streak down its nose. Holy Man stole some of the feathers of this bird to use for his ordinary arrows. The chief became angry because of this.

PLATE XI. *The Four Arrow People:* The four figures of this painting are Arrow People—the male at the south, of turquoise; the female above him, of whiteshell; the male next, of abalone; and the top female, of redstone. Each one carries in inverted position an arrow similar to its own body. These arrows represent the arrows which the Sun used in the sky, arrows too powerful and perishable to be entrusted into any hands but his own.

The protector at the feet of the turquoise Arrow Man is zigzag lightning; that of the white-shell Arrow Woman is rain streamer; that of abalone Arrow Man, flash lightning; and that of redstone Arrow Woman, a rainbow.

The tassels on the skirts and the pouches are very elaborate, but have no significance except that they indicate the generosity of the painters.

It is obvious that the bodies of the figures are arrows; not so apparent that the upstretched arms are bows—dark bows bound with red sinew for the males, yellow bows bound in white for the females. Each figure carries its corresponding bow in the left hand. The strings hanging down from the arms are otterskins.

Necks, face and head are identical in form and symbolism with those of Holy Man of Plate X, except that each Arrow wears the red bonnet, symbol of the Shooting Chant, in the dance representing it at the Corral Dance. It symbolizes the red afterglow of the setting sun.

White cornmeal is carried from the forehead to the chin of the Rainbow goddess. Unlike any other paintings of her, arms and legs are red and blue to correspond with the colors of the sides of her body.

This painting, the simplest arrangement, may be used in a one-night or five-night ceremony.

PLATE XII. *The Whiteshell Arrow People:* This and the preceding painting characterize a common method of representation. A picture for which less is paid, or one used in a short or unpretentious ceremony, is simple. One for which more is paid, or used when the ceremony is elaborated, is more complicated. It often has the figures arranged in quadrants separated by plants or some other symbol. In this case the plants are simply called black, blue, white and variegated (pink) herbs. Plants usually have three roots and five stems in the Shooting Chant.

Except for the protections of the feet which are moved up to the legs, the symbolism being the same, the Arrow figures are identical with those of Plate XI. Each stands on a short rainbow (sometimes called sundog). There is one other difference, which seems not to have a meaning, namely that the nocks of the arrows of Plate XI come above the shoulders, those of Plate XII below.

When the encircling guardian has bunches of five eagle, blue hawk, yellow hammer and magpie feathers at the four corners, instead of a head at the north and feet at the south, it indicates the rainbow garland instead of the goddess. The eastern guardians are a white and black Big Fly. The eastern guardians, and other parts of the paintings as well, are sometimes laid on pollen, a feature which is indicated by the yellow dots of the background.

This painting may be used as one of the main paintings (*i. e.*, on one of the last four days of the chant) and at the ceremony given by a medicine man to authorize his knowledge and ability to sing properly for others. (Plates XI and XII may be compared with Newcomb-Reichard, Plate XXXV).

PLATE XIII. *The Feathered Arrow People:* Since the arrows made of precious stones were too perishable to be given to Earth People, the Sun gave his sons, Holy Man and Holy Boy, substitutes. There were two male arrows, one called the eagle-feathered arrow because it had eagle feathers on both sides. The other was the yellow tail-feathered arrow which had eagle feathers on one side, the feathers of yellow-tailed hawk on the other. These are depicted as bodies in the figures at the east and south of the painting and in the right hands of the figures as well.

The female "arrows" were not arrowlike in appearance but are better described as "wands." They are always represented as are the wands in the right hands of the figures at west and north. However the bodies of the females are shaped like arrows. The wand belonging to Holy Woman had only eagle feathers, that belonging to Holy Girl had some red feathers amongst the eagle feathers. Arms of all figures, like those of Plates XI, XII represent bows, black for males, yellow for females. The nocks of the arrows, like those of Plate XII, are below the shoulders. All other parts of the figures are like, and mean the same thing, as corresponding parts of the arrow figures in Plate XII. The herbs at the corners and the guardians are also the same.

The blue center represents the water of the flood which caused the emergence from the underworld (the story not included in this legend), for the home of the Arrow People was called the Place-of-emergence-from-darkness. The ladder, as customarily, indicates the emergence of people from one world to another. The black circle around the blue center represents the darkness from which the people emerged; the white circle next it, the foam on the water; the yellow, pollen on the water; the red, the rainbow.

The small figure north of the ladder is the locust, with which arrows are identified, and the one south of the ladder is the grebe, the sacred pet of the chief of the Arrow People.

At each point of the compass next to the center are small rainbows and on each is a featherlike object. These represent the jeweled arrows, precious to the Sun, for which the Feathered Arrow People stand.

This picture may not be used at the installation of a medicine man.

Changing Woman and all her family, including Enemy Slayer, returned to their home at Whirling Mountain. Holy Man and Holy Boy set out over the mountain with their arrows. When they sighted some habitations, Holy Man said to his brother, "You had better go back home. I am going to see who lives there."

Holy Man arrived at Mountain-which-fell-out, the home of the Big Snakes. When he entered, Big Snake addressed him saying, "How are you, my son-in-law? Have you any tobacco?" Four times he asked and three times Holy Man said, "No." The fourth time Holy Man produced his tobacco pouch which had two compartments, one for ordinary tobacco and one for poisonous tobacco. Big Snake took one puff and fell over unconscious. His wife begged Holy Man to restore him. He said he would if she would pay him. She gave him beads and other valuables, and her husband was restored. This happened four times, and at the end Holy Man had all the treasures of the Big Snake.

Big Snake now bargained to get back some of his valuables and gave Holy Man five paintings:

There was a painting of the Big Snakes (Newcomb-Reichard, Plate VI) which was used as a first-aid painting and is a part of others which are more elaborate (Plate XIV at east).

A simple painting was that of four Crooked Snakes—a black one at the south; next to it, a white one; next that, a blue one; and finally, a yellow one.

PLATE XIV. *The Mountain-that-fell-out:* The place where the Snake People lived was called the Mountain-that-fell-out, because there was a mountain not attached to a chain or ridge, an odd mountain, as it were. The yellow circle represents the mountain home of the snakes and in the sandpainting is made to look like a hill by the piling up of sand. The red cross is the fire; the black circle, the smokehole. The surrounding outlines are: black for darkness; white for dawn, red-blue for rainbow. (These outlines are very common, and when they stand for "houses" are interpreted as here. When they surround "water," which may be a home also, the black [or blue] represents the water [or darkness as in Plate XIII]; the white, foam; the yellow, "real" or "water" pollen, that is, pollen from the cattail; and red-blue, the rainbow. Note that the one of the five colors which forms the ground of the design is always lacking in the outlines. *Author's note.*)

Short rainbows around the center house form platforms on which the People stand. In this case they are Snake People of all kinds: at east and west, the Big Snakes; at south, the Crooked Snakes; at the north, the straight or Arrowsnakes.

The Snakes are depicted as People, although they retain tails shown with rattles, and tongues shown as fangs. The marks on legs and bodies of the snakes are characteristic of the Shooting Chant. The small chevron on legs, arms and body indicates a deer track or hoof and is symbolical of prized flesh food. The small rectangle has been interpreted as the Snake's house or gait, and the curved marks in pairs are the phases of the moon, used in different positions according to the time of month and year when the painting is made, and changed also for the purpose of the chant (*i.e.*, whether it is according-to-holiness or evil-chasing). (It will be noticed that the moon phases are not used on the Arrow Snakes, and are similarly lacking on the Big Snakes of Newcomb-Reichard, Plate III. The use of these marks is not clear. *Author's note.*)

At the angles of the bodies of the Crooked Snakes there are small stripes of all the colors. They are arranged as are the outlines of centers (houses) relative to the background color. For example, if the background color is white, then the top stripe is black. Since the key color of the painting is female first (upper figure at east), the next outline color is yellow and it is paired with blue, then red follows making the rainbow at the bottom. The possibilities for variation in the arrangement of these colors are great and they are grouped differently for different chants, for different phases of a single chant, or for difference in sex of patients. The colors, however, are the usual symbols of the Shooting Chant: white for dawn, blue for sky, yellow for evening light, black for darkness; but when blue and red come together they stand for the rainbow, hence moisture.

The small white lines dropped from these stripes represent olivella shells which, in their turn, stand for rain.

The idea of plentiful flesh food is carried out in the deerhoof tassels of the skirt, the sash of deerhooves, and the ends of the pendent armstrings which are also deerhoof rattles.

Given the distinguishing features of the snakes, the rest of the body is similar to those described for other "people," Holy Man, for example, and the Arrow People. Matthews, in the Night Chant, p. 19, remarks that goddesses have square heads (or masks) while the heads of the gods are round. This may be true for the Night Chant but does not hold for the Shooting Chant as is evidenced by this painting. Here a female (white, yellow) stands at each point of the compass with a male (black, blue), yet the heads of all the Big Snakes are round, whereas those of the others are square. The word which has often been translated as "female" should better be rendered or thought of as "weaker, having less power," or even as "submissive." If we think of it that way, it is obvious that in some cases "female" will do, but this word does not cover enough. The Big Snakes dominate the others and that is the reason their heads are round.

The pairs of Snakes of this painting at east and west and at south and north respectively represent all the colors and the sexed pairs, as is evidenced by the objects they hold: the white females hold eagle-feathered wands; the yellow females, red-feathered wands; the black males, the eagle-feathered arrows; and the blue males, the yellow tail-feathered arrows. The females have yellow bows; the males dark bows.

The animal snakes at the corners and at the east are guards, and the Rainbow goddess in its usual form encircles the whole.

This painting may be used for a five-day or nine-day ceremony.

[52]

The fourth picture given at this time shows four Crooked Snake People standing in the four directions around a black circle which represents a lake. On it are four rainbows. The Crooked Snake at the east is black with outlines at the angles: white, blue, yellow, red. From these lines short white "rain" lines fall. In his left hand he carries the black sinew-wrapped bow, in his right, the white-feathered arrow. He wears the red bonnet on his head.

The blue Crooked Snake, at the south, is similar except that the outlines of his body are yellow, black, white, red; his arrow is the yellow tail-feathered arrow. Lightning protects both this and the black snake, which are males.

At the west the Crooked Snake is white with outlines: black, yellow, blue, red. It carries a yellow bow and the eagle-feathered wand.

The Crooked Snake at the north is yellow with blue, white, black, red outlines, and carries a yellow bow and the red-feathered wand. The two female snakes at west and north stand on small rainbows.

All the snakes in this painting differ from the ordinary Crooked Snakes in having only the deerhoof marks on the body.

At the corners of the picture blue corn grows to the southeast, blue bean to the southwest, black squash to the northwest, and black tobacco to the northeast.

A rainbow garland with bunches of five eagle, blue hawk, yellowhammer and magpie feathers encircles the picture from southeast to northeast. A crooked white snake is the eastern guard at the north, a black one at the south.

Holy Man learned the picture of the Red Snakes from Red Mountain at this time. This painting will be described later (Plate XIV, p. 56) to explain how it was used.

After giving Holy Man these paintings and receiving some of his own treasure as payment, Old Man Big Snake said, "I know but little. Over there at Sky-reaching-rock, the home of all the Snake People, lives their head and he knows everything. There is great danger in going there." He asked Holy Man to become his son-in-law and Holy Man stayed there all night. However his curiosity had been aroused and in the morning he started out for the tall rock.

On the way the Wind told him that there were two little sidewinders as guards of the tall rock, and gave Holy Man their names. Holy Man entered a house in the shape of a tall rock where it was completely dark. With the aid of a crystal which he carried with him he was able to see that all kinds of snakes except the watersnake—big snakes, arrowsnakes, and crooked snakes—were there. In the center corn with twelve ears on a stalk was growing.

The head of the snakes addressed him, "How are you, Holy Man? What are you doing here?"

"Nothing. I'm just looking around."

"Where were you last night?" asked the chief.

"Over at Big Snake's house."

"Ha! He is a tricky old fellow! What kind of a time did you have there?"

Then Holy Man told all that happened and explained the rites and paintings he had learned from Snake Man.

When he had finished the Snake chief said, "Is that all? Wouldn't he give you any more?"

"No, he said that was all he knew."

"He only gave you the unimportant first-aid painting. I will teach you the important ones."

He then made and explained the painting of the Snake People and the Corn.

This is the painting of Newcomb-Reichard Plate III and is considered the key painting of the Snake group. It is used in the nine-day Sun's House performance of the Chant. It shows the importance of corn and domesticated plants in connection with the power of the Snakes over flesh food as represented by the symbols on their bodies, the deerhoof tassels and rattles.

Holy Man went back to Old Man Big Snake's house and was asked, "Where have you been, my son-in-law?"

Holy Man said, "At Red Mountain."

"Didn't I tell you it was dangerous to go there? Those people do not tell the truth."

Holy Man had seen a speck moving far off as he traveled and asked Big Snake what it was. "Never mind what it was. Dangers are so great you do not want to know such things."

This reply only confirmed Holy Man in his intention to find out and he started off the next morning. The Wind once more whispered the names of the four guards, and Holy Man passed them safely to find still another Snake home. This place was called Grinding Snakes and he saw many snakes grinding herbs on twelve huge metates. Their head was another Big Snake who spoke to him, "Where are you going, Holy Man?"

"Nowhere. I'm just looking around."

"Where were you last night?"

Holy Man told him. Then he asked what that was moving far off on the horizon. This time Big Snake told him it was the Endless Snake. At this place Holy Man learned the pictures of the Grinding Snakes and of the Endless Snake.

PLATE XV. *The Grinding Snakes:* This painting is rarely used because it is numbered among the most precious of all the paintings, and is the rarest of all the Snake paintings. It may be made if the patient is a young man or a young woman, a member of an unusually wealthy or important family. The medicine man who furnishes the painting receives an extra high fee, and paints it on the last day of a nine-night performance.

If this painting is to be used the ceremony may be planned for as long as a year in advance. All the singers of the Shooting Chant are invited to attend. Large quantities of herbs are gathered from which dry medicine is mixed and blessed on this painting. The chanters then use this medicine later in connection with lesser paintings and rites. It is greatly cherished and sparingly used since years may pass before an opportunity arises to replenish the supply.

The black square in the center represents a metate, the blue bar outlined with yellow is the grinding stone or mano. The rainbows on it symbolize the power (endurance) of the hands which use the stone. The twelve snakes at each side represent twelve brothers who had magic hunting power, and they refer also to the twelve Medicine People of Figure 3. These snakes are significant of flesh and vegetable food supply and this is once more emphasized by the stalks of corn growing from the corners of the *metate*. The blackbird, blue swallow, bluebird and oriole, mounted on the black, blue, white and yellow corn respectively, confer blessing on the food.

The figures on the rainbow rafts are Crooked Snake People at east and west, Arrowsnake People at south and north, and are identical with those of Plate XIV except that they carry corn in the right hand and a basket in the left. The basket, being either of whiteshell or turquoise, corresponds in color with the person who holds it, fortuitously when a white snake holds the whiteshell basket, or a blue snake holds one of turquoise.

Small snakes between the People and the corn of corresponding color are guards as are the little animal snakes at the east. The rainbow garland is the protecting "string" or "rope."

This picture is to be compared with a similar one in Newcomb-Reichard, Plate IX in which all the figures are Crooked Snakes, holding bows and arrows. The center is a black square, said to be the Snakes' home. On it a white bar represents the *metate* and the rainbows the *manos*. The bodies of the snakes are said to be interlaced underneath their home because they are moving it. At the corners are herbs and there are no small animal guards between them and the People. A remark in the notes comparing the twelve snakes with the twelve Medicine People of Figure 3 suggests that this picture refers to the Sun's gift of medicine to his children (p. 44).

With the exception of the eastern guardians which are in both cases sidewinders, the color symbolism is the same in both paintings of the Grinding Snakes.

The painting of the Endless Snake which Holy Man learned at this time is identical with that of Newcomb-Reichard, Plate XII.

"This is symbolical of the power of all the Snake People. The black color indicates the darkness of the spirit world whence the Navajo emerged. The deerhoof marks on the body symbolize the paths of life, as well as plentiful game supply.

"The four smaller coiled snakes are guardians, the black one guards the sky, the white one the earth, the blue one the mountains, the yellow one the waters."

After learning the secrets and powers of the snakes at Grinding Snake Place, Holy Man returned to the house of Old Man Big Snake, who scolded him for disobeying and once more asked him to marry his daughter. But again Big Snake aroused Holy Man's curiosity by telling him about Striped Mountain which, he said, was a very dangerous place. Of course the hero started off the next morning to visit it. The Wind told him the names of the guards and he reached the place in safety.

Upon arrival he found various kinds of reptiles, water snakes, arrowsnakes with striped bodies, certain lizards, and the horned worm as well. Here he learned the painting of the Snakes with Striped Bodies.

This is the painting of Newcomb-Reichard, Plate VII. All the figures are Arrowsnakes, but Big Snakes or Crooked Snakes may be used.

These snakes taught Holy Man how to make prayersticks for the holiness phase and hoops for the evil-chasing phase of the Shooting Chant, as well as the songs and prayers that go with them.

Holy Man now returned to Old Man Big Snake's house and decided to marry his daughter. The next morning his father-in-law warned him against going to a red mountain which they could see in the distance because it was exceptionally dangerous. This was just the thing Holy Man needed to make him want to investigate and he started off. On the way he met a red coyote from that place for, just as the mountain was red, so were all the animals and people who lived there.

Red Coyote had wanted to marry Big Snake's daughter and now that he had heard Holy Man had her, he was very jealous. When he met Holy Man he blew his own skin onto his rival, transforming him into a coyote, and he himself took on the form and appearance of Holy Man. In this form Red Coyote went to Big Snake's house and was addressed as "My son-in-law." But the daughter said, "No, this is not Holy Man, my husband. This is Red Coyote. I can smell him." The Wind had whispered the secret to her.

During this time Holy Man's family had missed him and had sent a coyote from Whirling Mountain to search for him. The people of Big Snake's family, including his new wife, also went out to hunt for him. They followed Holy Man's tracks until the end where they found a coyote curled up in a place over which willows and a wildrose had grown together. They brought Holy Man back and with him four branches of the willow and one from the wildrose. These they used for making five prayerhoops for restoration. They had facets cut out and painted to look like faces. They were so made that when the sacred string with which they were bound was pulled, they would spring open and look like the snakes they represented. The Arrowsnakes had taught Holy Man how to make the hoops. One painted white to which an eagle feather was tied was set at the east; a blue one with a bluebird feather to the south; a yellow one with a canary feather to the west; and a black one with a turkey feather to the north.

The first day they pushed Holy Man through the first hoop and the skin cracked over his head. The next day they put him through the second hoop and the skin came down to his shoulders. The third day as he was taken through the third hoop, the skin came down to his hips; and on the fourth it fell to his ankles. Then the thorns of the wildrose hoop pulled it off entirely and Holy Man had human form, but had not recovered his senses.

The people in attendance had exhausted their powers and sent for help to the chief of the people living at Sky-reaching-rock. With paintings and rites they restored his speech. Runners went to Grinding Snakes and Endless Snake and these people succeeded in restoring the hearing of the afflicted man. Other messengers ran to Striped Mountain and people living there restored his sight.

Meanwhile Holy Man's relatives held a council to consider how they would restore his health, for he was very thin and all his flesh seemed shriveled up. The people whom they called "see-ers" had heard that the Eagle People could do so. They sent for Black Hawks and Turkey Buzzards who performed their rites in vain.

Among the Eagle People were the star gazers who told them that the People at Red Mountain could restore Holy Man's health. All of the people assembled and sent for the powers who lived at Red Mountain. These people, like the coyote from there, were red all over. They performed their ceremony with its painting and succeeded in restoring Holy Man to health.

PLATE XVI. *The Red Snake People from Red Mountain:* This effective painting is a companion picture to Plate XIV. The story relates the great danger Holy Man was in, and the red (covering the mountain home as well as the snakes) indicates danger also. It is a picture of the evil-chasing phase of the Shooting Chant. The center corresponds to the yellow mountain home of Mountain-fallen-out, and black circle and cross indicate home, smokehole and fire as they did there; but now red covers all. The encircling outlines of Sky protectors are the same as they were, but since red is the ground color, yellow changes places with it and is outside. The fact that red is in the center indicates danger—instead of protection, as it does when it is outside.

Except that the bodies of the snakes are red, they are identical with those of Plate XIV. They are to be recognized by the fact that their outline colors are preserved. For instance, white snake is outlined in black, the white body is covered with red and the black remains; black snake outlined in white retains the white outline when its body becomes red.

Instead of the pair of animal snake guardians which fill the corners of Plate XIV, the Red Snakes stand between the domesticated plants: blue corn with the sacred bird at the southeast, blue bean at the southwest, black squash at northwest and blue tobacco at northeast. The drawing of tobacco does not differ from that of other herbs, but the representation means the tobacco plant only when it is used with the other domesticated plants.

This painting may be used when a person is ill because of contact with evil or evil influences, and such are indefinite, intangible causes for illness due to witchcraft rather than to the breaking of a taboo or the ceremonial performance of something out of order.

VII

Legend and Sandpaintings of the Male Shooting Chant: Encounters with Sky and Buffalo People

THE NEXT DAY HOLY MAN AND HIS FAMILY all left Big Snake's home. Holy Man left his Snake wife and started up Black Mountain. He had by this time been reunited with his brother, Holy Boy, and said to him, "Let us go hunting. I will start up Black Mountain on this side and you go toward Mt. Taylor, then we shall meet at White Rock between the two mountains."

Holy Man started up Black Mountain and before long saw a mountain sheep. He headed it off and found ambush on the top of the mountain where a Douglas fir and a blue spruce grew in a clump of oaks. He hid under the oaks and shot at the mountain sheep from there. It fell between the fir and spruce. The arrow he used was one feathered with the plumage of the grebe which Holy Man had stolen from the chief of the Locust People. He skinned the sheep at once cutting it open at the breast. It was very fat and he put a piece of the fat in his mouth. Meanwhile clouds had gathered near him and he had not noticed the weather.

Suddenly two streaks of lightning flashed from the clouds striking Holy Man and the fir trees. All the leaves were stripped from the trees. Holy Man was wearing the skin of an otter over his shoulders. This deflected the lightning which ran down to his feet picking him up and carrying him to the home of the Thunders in the sky.

Because Holy Man had used the feathers of the white-nosed bird without permission, his father, the Sun, and the Sky People were angry. They had told the Thunders to send lightning to bring him to the sky where they would reprimand him and instruct him more thoroughly in the use of his power.

At the home of the Thunders there was a lake in the center. A black Thunder sat at the east, a blue Thunder at the west, a variegated Thunder at the south and a "left-handed" Thunder at the north. Wind told Holy Man that White Thunder had brought him there. Near the lake was a sandpainting of the Home of the Thunder People.

The Home of the Thunder People is nearly the same as the painting of Newcomb-Reichard, Plate XXXI. The black center circle represents a lake with four rainbows and the outlines are of white, which means foam; yellow for pollen; and red-blue for rainbow. Whereas the plate referred to has black corn, beans, squash and tobacco at the four corners, the Huckel painting has corn corresponding in color to the colors of the nearest Thunders: black at the east, yellow (for variegated) at the south, blue at the west, pink at the north. Since pink is used for white when Thunders are concerned, the corn at the northeast belonging to Pink Thunder is white.

In this painting zigzag lightnings connect the feet of Black Thunder at the east and Yellow Thunder at the south; rain streamers run from the left to the right foot of the Blue and Pink Thunders respectively. In the Newcomb-Reichard painting these symbols run outward from each foot instead of connecting them. Big Flies are guardians of the east. The Huckel painting has no guardians.

FIGURE 6. *Holy Man Captured by the Thunders:* In this picture Holy Man is shown in the power of the Thunders, a black one at the east, a yellow one at the south, a blue one at the west and a

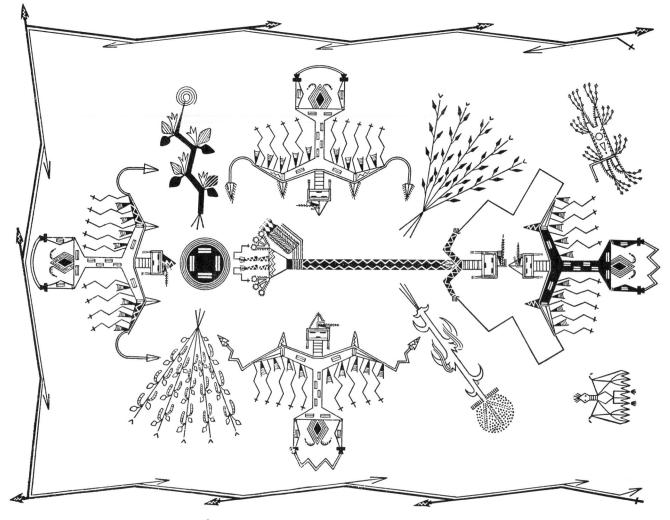

FIGURE 6. HOLY MAN CAPTURED BY THE THUNDERS

pink one at the north. This is one of the two paintings combined for the so-called "double" painting (see p. 62), but differs from it slightly in composition. In the double sandpainting Holy Man is attached to all the Thunders by lightnings, sunbeams and rain streamers; here zigzag lightnings run from his hands to the tips of Dark Thunder's wings only.

Near the feet of Holy Man is the lake near which the Thunders live. On it are four rainbows and around it the colors which usually add power to water. From it grow the four domesticated plants: blue corn and bean, black squash and tobacco.

Black and white zigzag lightnings form the encircling guardian and Sun's tobacco pouch and Bat guard the east.

Black Thunder came and made a motion from the east toward the center of the picture, then from the west, the south and the north. Then, as he made a pass toward the center of the picture, it disappeared and in its place there was nothing but a deep hole. This hole was the entrance to the House of Big Thunder.

Across the entrance hole were four guards: zigzag lightning, sheet lightning, sunbeam and rainbow. A ladder of zigzag lightning led down into the hole. At its foot sat Big Thunder.

Front cover, FIGURE 7. *Big Thunder:* Big Thunder is symbolical of all thunder and just as the Place-of-emergence is considered black as the origin of people, so Big Thunder is black as the origin of all his kind.

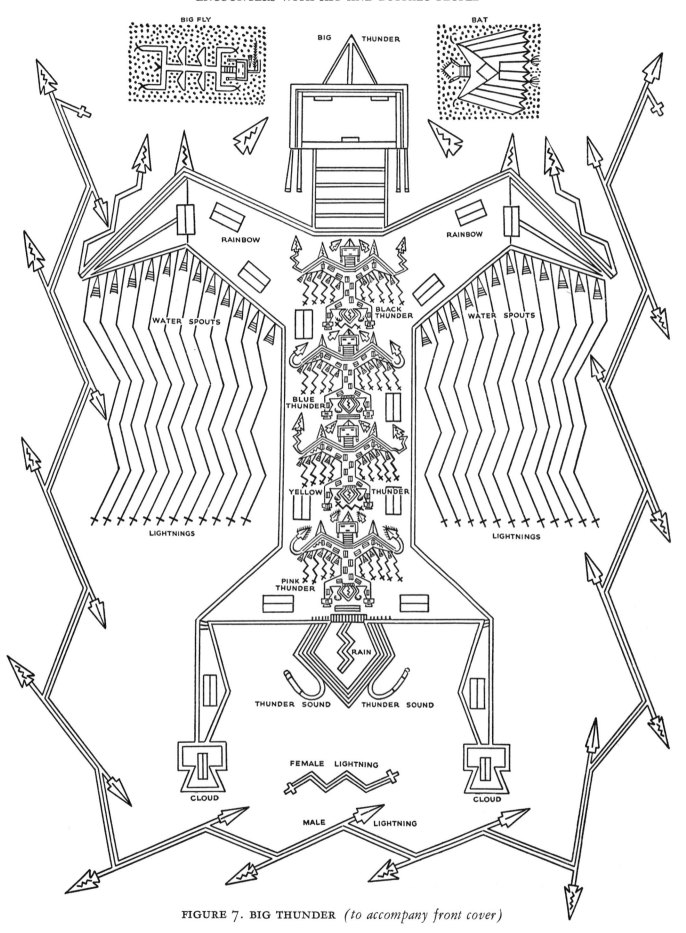

FIGURE 7. BIG THUNDER *(to accompany front cover)*

[59]

The body of Thunder is birdlike except for the neck and face. The shape of the legs with calves (if they may be so called) turned inward shows the personage sitting like a bird. The feet are clouds with superimposed rainbows. The lozenge-shaped tail, sometimes black and sometimes brown, is thought of as carrying rain, represented by zigzag or straight lines, usually in four colors. The curves at the ends of the tail, usually pink with black or white tips, represent the thunder's reverberation.

Short rainbows are set at various points of the body of Thunder. The wing tips are of a color contrasting with that of the body, usually the color of the Thunder placed opposite. For instance, black Thunder has blue wing tips, blue Thunder has black wing tips, yellow Thunder has pink wing tips and pink Thunder has wing tips of yellow. The aid given by one to the opposite one of the pair is thus symbolized.

From each wing of Big Thunder hang twelve waterspouts which correspond in color and shape with the headfeather from the bundle of the Shooting Chant, and alternating with them are twelve lightnings. The number twelve is idealized, as are other parts of Big Thunder, for most thunders of the Shooting Chant have nine waterspouts and nine lightnings subtly arranged in groups of five or four.

Thunders are provided with arrows which extend above the wings, at the wing tips and at the top of the head. The face is like that of other "people" of the Shooting Chant.

On the body of the great Thunder are four imitations of him in black, blue, yellow and pink. Their symbolism is the same, but the number of waterspouts and lightnings is smaller.

Zigzag lightnings, Big Fly and Bat are the guards.

This painting may be used only for one who has been struck by lightning or injured in a storm. Special long prayersticks, the peculiar offering demanded by the Thunder gods, must be used with this painting.

Big Thunder seemed very angry at Holy Man and said to his four companions, "Why do you bring Earth People into my house?"

In the east were Sky People on top of a black cloud; in the west, Water People on a blue cloud; in the south, Sun People on a yellow cloud; in the north, Summer People on a pink cloud. The Sky People answered Big Thunder, "Perhaps he came back for something."

There was a Big Fly who always stayed with Big Thunder, and of course Holy Man's Big Fly was with him. They consulted in whispers, "Who is this and where did he come from?" The Big Fly from the earth answered, "He is Holy Man, originally from the Place-of-emergence and later from Whirling Mountain. His mother is Changing Woman, his father is the Sun."

Big Thunder's Fly then whispered to him, "This is Holy Man." "So-o!" said Big Thunder. Then he addressed Holy Man, "The Sun instructed you in the way of the gods but you have disobeyed. For that reason you have been brought before me for further instructions in the ways of the Holy Ones."

Big Thunder then turned to his assistants and asked, "Are there any others?"

They answered, "Yes, there are people here from the Female and the Mountain Shooting Chants, others from the Wind Chant and the Water and Hail Chants."

Here it is that some of the other chants are connected with the Male Shooting Chant.

A picture almost identical with that of Newcomb-Reichard Plate XIV belongs here. There are slight differences in the protectors of the feet of the four figures, Holy Man, Holy Woman, Holy Boy and Holy Girl. Those of Holy Man and Holy Boy are black lightnings; in Newcomb-Reichard they are black and white. Holy Woman and Holy Girl stand on short rainbows; in Newcomb-Reichard, rain streamers curve off from each foot of Holy Woman, rainbows from those of Holy Girl. The eastern guardians of the Huckel picture are white and black Big Flies; those of the Newcomb-Reichard picture are Sun and Moon.

These two paintings are an excellent illustration of the slight changes which may distinguish certain phases of a chant. In the Huckel picture Holy Man stands for Rainboy because the picture is used most frequently as a first-aid painting of the Hail Chant. It represents the substitution of

Rainboy, the hero of the Hail Chant, for Holy Man. The only way such a difference could be known is from the minute description of the medicine man who knows the legends and the points at which the mythology overlaps.

Another painting in the Huckel Collection has the protectors of the feet exactly as the one in Newcomb-Reichard, Plate XIV, but depicts the body paintings on the chest and arms in great detail. The figures all wear the red feather bonnet lacking in the other two paintings, and Sun and Moon are the eastern guardians.

This painting is believed to have been given to Holy Man by the Sun at Black Rock somewhat later in his adventures (see p. 67), but it is described here because it is so nearly like the other two.

When all had come in, Big Thunder taught them about the use of the prayersticks, prayer hoops, herbs and paintings, and drilled them in the accompanying prayers and songs. Some of the Thunder People who had followed Holy Man to the sky were given orders, and after Big Thunder had finished, they brought Holy Man back to earth at the top of Black Mountain.

During the four-day absence of Holy Man, Changing Woman and Monster Slayer had prayed for his safety. Monster Slayer had made the painting of Holy Man protected by Monster Slayer and Child-of-the-water (Plate X).

When Holy Man had returned in safety Monster Slayer asked him where he had been and what had become of his brother, Holy Boy. Holy Man gave the story of his adventures. "When we started out I told him to meet me at White Rock," he said. "But of course because of my capture by the Thunders I was not able to get there myself."

Big Fly took the news of Holy Boy's absence to Talking God and *xactcé'óɣan* at the Stone-bridge-where-two-rivers-meet. They came and joined the council. Talking God was somewhat miffed and asked why he had not been sent for. What had he done that he should be thus ignored? The people said that they were sorry, but they had not thought to implore him, but now they were glad he had come. They gave him a buckskin, and to *xactcé'óɣan*, an otterskin, symbols which are always associated with these gods.

The painting of Holy Boy protected by Talking God and *xactcé'óɣan* was then laid (Plate XX). Talking God prayed to the people of the bottom of the waters, thus showing he knew where Holy Boy was although he did not tell the people directly. After the rites were over he told them to go search for Holy Boy.

When the two boys had started off hunting Holy Boy had gone toward the top of Mt. Taylor where there was a lake. After leaving his brother he came around the mountain to the White Rock where he was to meet his brother. Not finding him, he started off for the top of the mountain. As he passed Mountain-fallen-out, the guards of the Snake's house, mistaking him for his brother, Holy Man, said to him, "Where are you going?" "Just wandering around," he answered.

He went on and came to a meadow at the foot of the mountain where the Big Black Ants lived. He stopped for a time watching their games and races, then went on. He next came to a lake on the side of the mountain, a beautiful place where all kinds of plants grew around the edge. Another group of ants lived there, and their chief asked where he was going. "Just wandering about," he said.

"But where did you come from my grandchild? It is only proper to tell where you are from."

Then Holy Boy told him he was from Whirling Mountain, and the chief gave him white, blue, yellow and shining plants to use as medicine.

Holy Boy went on and when he looked across Black Mountain he saw a heavy thunderstorm, the Thunders taking his brother to the sky, although of course he did not know it. At the top of a hill he found a pond only a few feet in diameter, a pool which expanded and receded. Near the center was a cornstalk and near it floated two eagle feathers. Holy Boy was now overcome with a desire to have the eagle feathers. He reached for the cornstalk from the east side, but could not quite touch it. He tried from the west, south and north, but missed it every time. Once more he reached for the cornstalk from the east, thinking to steady himself as he tried for the feathers, but he lost his balance and fell in. A huge fish was waiting there for him. It swallowed him at once and took him to Whirling Waters at the bottom of the lake.

A search party led by Holy Man started out to find the brother. They tracked him to White Rock where Spider Man said he had seen Holy Boy pass by. At Mountain-fallen-out the Snakes said they had spoken to him as he passed. The Ant People said he had passed there about noon. The party came to the lake where Holy Boy had received the healing herbs, and thence tracked him to the edge of the small lake at the top of the mountain, where the trail disappeared.

Here they gave the ducks on the lake offerings of precious stones to look for Holy Boy in the water. The ducks could not see him and said he must still be somewhere out on the plains.

Then Wolf went through the valleys inquiring of everyone he could see but could find no trace of the lost boy. The people called upon Yellow Thunder who lived on top of Sky-reaching-rock. He looked in the clouds and could find no clue. Then Bear was asked to search the caves and canyons of the mountain and he also failed to find a trace.

After Holy Boy was swallowed by the Big Fish, which was transparent, he passed four habitations of Water People. At the Place-of-the-big-reeds the turtles lived. The Turtle spoke to Holy Boy saying, "When you come back stop here."

They next reached the place called White Waters where the white fish lived. Then they came to Dividing Waters where the water oxen lived. They had the same colors as the Thunders. The third place the travelers reached was the home of the Monster Fish Maidens and at last they came to the home of the Big Fish. At each place they had spent a night.

The search party led by Holy Man had finally come back to the lake where they had lost the tracks of Holy Boy. He decided his brother must be in the water and threw in offerings of precious stones.

At that very moment Holy Boy remembered the string of flint points he had long since obtained from the cedar waxwing, and which still hung around his neck. With them he cut his way out of the fish. Then he used the herbs he had secured from the Ant People to heal the cut made in the fish.

The chief of the Deep Water People then said to the Big Fish who had swallowed Holy Boy, "What do you mean by bringing an Earth person down here?" Then a Big Fish Maiden spoke for him, "That is Holy Boy, son of Changing Woman and the Sun." A Big Water Fly had told her this.

The Big Fish then explained how Holy Boy had been captured. First the Black Fish had tried to get him when he reached for the feathers from the east, then Yellow Fish tried it from the west, Blue Fish from the south and White Fish from the north.

The painting called Sky-reaching-rock is also called the double sandpainting. It is among the most detailed and elaborate of the pictures. It was published in color in *Spider Woman*[1] and in outline form by Newcomb-Reichard.[2] The picture at the north is similar to Figure 6 which shows Holy Man in the power of the Thunders. The picture at the south represents Holy Boy taken captive by Fish. All the places concerned in the two episodes are depicted: Sky-reaching-rock; Black Mountain, where Holy Man shot the mountain sheep with the grebe-feathered arrow; and Mt. Taylor where Holy Boy tried to get the feathers from the pond. All the creatures which helped in the search for him—ducks, Wolf, Yellow Thunder, and Bear—are shown. I do not think the picture of Holy Boy captured by the Fish is ever used by itself, although Holy Man in the home of the Thunders may be (Figure 6).

The painting of Sky-reaching-rock in the Huckel Collections has a black circle within a yellow circle and on it a cross, again to represent smokehole and fire. This use is characteristic of the

[1] Gladys A. Reichard, Macmillan, New York, 1934.

[2] *Sandpaintings of the Navajo Shooting Chant*, figure 3, p. 20.

version used for the Fire Dance form of the chant. A spotted circle around the yellow represents moss. In other respects the picture is the same as the one previously published.

(At a Shooting Chant with Fire Dance given in November, 1938 I saw this picture again. It was like the one in the Huckel Collections except that it had two guardian ropes instead of the Rainbow around both pictures. The rainbow garland extended from southeast to the middle of the west side. From there to the northeast the lightning chain—black and white with white outside—was strung. *Author's note.*)

The god of the waters then proceeded to show Holy Boy the paintings of the Water People and taught him the offerings, prayers and songs.

FIGURE 8. THE WATER PEOPLE

FIGURE 8. *The Water People:* This, one of the most elaborate paintings of the Shooting Chant, depicts many of the powers of underwater forces. The black center represents a lake, around it are four black mountains on each of which is a dragonfly, the symbol of pure water. From these grow blue corn and bean, black squash and blue tobacco.

In each quarter formed by the plants a Thunder occupies the center of the space: black at the east, yellow at the south, blue at the west, and pink at the north. The thunders correspond with those described for the frontispiece, and in addition each is provided with the waterspout head bundle.

[63]

At the right of each thunder is one of the Water Oxen, whose body somewhat resembles that of Thunder. Instead of wings it has arms and there are horns on the head. In the right hand each carries an ear of corn of corresponding color and a magic hoop dangles from its wrist. A waterjar is hung from the left wrist of each of these persons. The black Water Ox holds five zigzag lightnings in his left hand, the blue one opposite has five flash lightnings. The yellow Water Ox at the south holds five sunbeams, and the pink one at the north holds five rainbows with serrated arrowpoints.

The animal at the left of each Thunder is a Water Horse, another of the water monsters. It looks much like a buffalo (cp. Plates XXIII, XXIV and Figure 9), carries a traveling hoop and a waterjar, and has rainbows at its feet which are clouds. The body is also covered with rainbows. The line running from mouth to heart represents the life of the animal, and the cranklike arrangement on the back symbolizes escape or restoration from danger, and consequent power to protect from danger.

All the birds are swallows.

Lightning encircles the picture. Beaver guards the east at the north, otter at the south.

In this picture the powers of moisture from the sky, lakes, mountains, and subterranean waters are represented (cp. Newcomb-Reichard, Plate XXXIII).

Meanwhile all the Water People had received a share of the offerings which Holy Man had thrown into the lake. They told him he could now return to the earth, but added instructions, "In case anyone has an accident or illness due to water, resuscitate such a person by making a painting of us, the Water People."

Then Holy Boy started back to earth. Mounted on a zigzag lightning he reached the home of the Monster Fish Maidens. From there he traveled on a straight lightning to the home of the Water Horses. He made the next lap to the home of the Turtles on a long rainbow. The Turtles, who had asked him to stop, gave him prayersticks, healing herbs and songs of the Water People. From their home he reached the top of the water on a short rainbow. From there he returned to Whirling Mountain with Changing Woman and the people who had come with her searching for her son.

When they got back, Talking God and *xactčé'óɣan* performed a one-night ceremony with one painting (presumably that of the Water People), prayers and thanks for Holy Boy's safe return.

Now, due to their various trying and strenuous experiences, Holy Man and Holy Boy were not in the best of health. They were thin and tired, having lost the tremendous energy which had previously consumed them. The people held a meeting and decided to hold the ceremony of the Shooting Chant with the Fire or Corral Dance feature on the last of the nine nights. It was decided that the medicine man in charge should be the chief of all the snakes from Sky-reaching-rock.

On the first day the small paintings of Holy Man protected by Monster Slayer and Child-of-the-water, and its companion picture with Holy Boy in the center (Plate X) were used.

On the second day they used the painting of the House-of-moving-points.

PLATE XVII. *The House-of-moving-points:* This picture represents the maximum of power secured by flint armor, increased because of the manifold repetition. The center gives the name to the picture and distinguishes it from Plates XVIII and XIX. The painting represents the new home of Changing Woman made for her by the Sun. (One of the main themes in Gray Eyes' narrative is the struggle of the Sun, aided by his children, to get Changing Woman to move from her old home which they considered sordid, to the beautiful new one Sun had made for her at the west. I find it curious that Miguelito never indicates this struggle although this picture and that of Plate XIX certainly refer to it. Compare Newcomb-Reichard, Plate XVII. *Author's note.*)

The center represents the house of Changing Woman protected by points which move so as to prevent the ingress of evil. Flint points are charms—material as well as figurative—against danger in any case, but motion makes them even more formidable. From the corners extend five black zigzag lightnings, five yellow sunbeams, five red-blue flash lightnings and five rainbows with serrated points. The protectors at the feet of the corresponding figures are the same, but add the weak or "submissive" (female) aid because they end in a cross instead of in barbed points.

The major figures stand on short rainbows.

The figures of Monster Slayer and Child-of-the-water are painted in the conventional style when armed as in Plate X. Almost never can one say that one figure is the same as another without exception. In these paintings the clothes and arms are the same even to the number of lightnings in the hands, darting from the bundle, and on the head. But the figures of Plate XVII have additional accouterments, the pendent strings of otterskin from the arms, and from the left hand the war shield and the Sun's tobacco pouch.

The shields in the shape of a star with seven points outside and five within show by their background color to whom they belong and by the inside design the protection of their opposites, black with blue inside, for instance, and blue ground with black inside.

The red object in the left hand of each figure represents a tobacco pouch elaborately embroidered in porcupine quills. The blue circle is the Sun, the blue triangular object near it, his tobacco pipe with a bit of tobacco in black at the mouthpiece, a white line indicating a smoke on the bowl. Monster Slayer, the black figure, and the blue Child-of-the-water carry the Sun's pouch. The yellow figure, Reared-within-the-mountain, and Changing Grandchild who is pink, carry the Moon's tobacco pouch.

The Sun and Moon are the eastern guardians.

On the third day the painting of the Four Mountains was used.

PLATE XVIII. *The Four Mountains:* This is a companion picture to Plates XVII and XIX and differs only in the center which depicts another phase of the home of the Holy Twins (or of their mother, Changing Woman). The four mountains in the center represent the place where spruce grew down the sides of the mountains. In the actual sandpainting the mountains are heaped up with sand and real sprigs of Colorado blue spruce and Douglas fir are planted on them.

As the lightnings of Plate XVII signify the warlike phase and protection of the wonderful home, so the plants growing from the center of this painting indicate the healing or spiritual aspect. The plants have their origin (white roots) in the moisture of the mountains.

PLATE XIX. *The House-of-many-points:* This painting is first mentioned later in the legend (p. 67) but it is explained here because it is so nearly like the two which precede it. Once more it is the center which varies. The black center represents the center mountain of the mythological universe. The black-blue subdivision is the house of Changing Woman fortified by the powerful flint of her children, the twin War Gods.

Changing Woman had charge of moisture and from her mountain home domesticated plants arise, all blue except the black squash. The corn has an oriole on its tip. As the House-of-moving-points signifies military protection, and the Four Mountains stand for healing and protection over supernatural affairs, so the domesticated plants indicate power over subsistence or material things.

The Shooting Chant, to demonstrate its complete potency, should be given four times for a patient. Any of the three paintings, Plates XVII, XVIII, or XIX, may be used at one ceremony, but not more than one. Anyone of the others may be, but do not have to be, used at subsequent ceremonies. The choice of paintings depends upon circumstances such as the wealth and wishes of the patient, the taste of the chanter, the length and purpose of the ceremony, and other factors.

A simpler version of the armed War Gods corresponds in every respect with that of Newcomb-Reichard, Plate XVI, except that every face has the symbol of Monster Slayer, five zigzag lightnings on the right cheek (Newcomb-Reichard, Plate XV). Since the four figures are in a row, the house is not shown. This painting is on the wall over the fireplace in the lobby of El Navajo Hotel.

On the fourth day Holy Man and Holy Boy protected by Talking God and *xactčé'óɣan* were represented in sand.

PLATE XX. *Holy Girl Protected by Talking God and xactčé'óɣan:* Since the ceremony was being performed for males, the picture of Holy Man was used, but since Holy Man was shown in Plate X,

Holy Girl was chosen for representation here. Just as the same symbol is used for Holy Man and Holy Boy (the kind of arrow indicating which is meant), so the same variegated figure is used for Holy Woman and Holy Girl. Since Holy Woman carries the eagle-feathered (white) wand, this figure with the red-feathered wand is Holy Girl.

The figure of Holy Girl represents the weaker contrast to Holy Man in all respects. At her feet is a rainbow as contrasted with the zigzag lightning of Holy Man, on her legs and arms is straight lightning where he has zigzag lightning, in her left hand the yellow bow, and in her right the red-feathered wand, weaker forms of the dark bow and eagle-feathered arrow, respectively.

The body of Holy Woman or Holy Girl is always variegated, but it is not usual to find either with this tapering shape. More commonly—and I have even seen Miguelito make them so—they are rectangular as in Newcomb-Reichard, Plates XIV, XXVII.

The painting of Plate X contrasts with this one in that it is used to drive off evil, since Monster Slayer and Child-of-the-water were concerned with ridding the world of evil. Talking God and *xactčé'óɣan*, on the other hand, are concerned primarily with bringing good, and that is why they are used here in the Fire Dance form of the ceremony.

The white figure at the left of Holy Girl is Talking God. This is the god who gives his name, Grandfather-of-the-gods, to the Night Chant, and in it he appears with a mask. He is the god of dawn and of the eastern sky. The twelve eagle feathers on his head represent the white light of predawn. His mask is the only white one used in the Night Chant.[1] The face in the painting is therefore white. The yellow designs at each side of the eagle feathers on the head represent bunches of owl feathers on the mask. He often carries his special talisman, a bag made of Abert's squirrel skin, but in this picture both he and his companion carry a pair of "talking prayersticks," the prayersticks given Holy Man by the Sun (p. 43) which were used to lead the one who had been turned into a coyote through the restorative hoops.

The companion of Talking God, *xactčé'óɣan*, whose name cannot be translated (it is not House God as Matthews has it[2]), is a farm god and a god of healing, the god of the west and the sunset, in all ways complementary to Talking God. The details of his costume correspond to those of Talking God except that his color is blue.

On the fifth day they used the painting of the Water People (Figure 8). The first five paintings had been used as "prayer" paintings, that is, the patients had sat on them while long prayers were intoned, a special way of using sandpaintings (see p. 22).

The people had decided to have the fullest kind of performance, and on the fifth night included the painting which goes with the Shock-caused-by-fear and its rites. Usually Holy Man accompanies the Bear in this rite, but since he was the patient, Rainboy took his place (see p. 15).

PLATE XXI. *The Shock Painting:* Occasionally when a very complete ceremony has been agreed upon, the rite of the Shock-caused-by-bear is given. Since Holy Man was learning everything, it was performed for him on the fifth day. The painting was made in sand and the patient sat on it. Then one person dressed as a bear and one impersonating Holy Man (in this case Rainboy as a substitute) rushed in and frightened the patient into a fainting fit. The chanter and all concerned then proceeded to restore the afflicted, after which he would no longer fear anything natural or supernatural.

The four white tracks leading to the painting signify the tracks of white cornmeal made by Changing Woman when Holy Man returned from the Sun's House.

The base of the painting is a rainbow. The tracks on the black background are bear tracks. The Big Black Snake, used when the patient is a man, has the markings described for Big Snakes (p. 52): rectangular figure for snake's house, chevron for deerhoof or game, curved lines for moon phases. The dots on the body may be made or omitted. They seem to have no meaning.

"The blue on the neck of the snake represents earthy things and people; the red bands, the breath or life.

The spruce twigs around the snake stand for the Dark-circle-of-branches of the Fire Dance.

When the Shock picture is used for a woman patient, the snake is white.

[1] Matthews, Washington. *The Night Chant,* p. 9. American Museum of Natural History, New York, 1902.
[2] *Idem,* p. 10.

Upon consultation the people had decided to invite all of the Earth and Sky People to participate in the dance of the last night. Two Rainboys were chosen as couriers to the Sky People and Holy Woman and Holy Girl were to invite the Earth People. These messengers had dots painted on their bodies, and wide stripes of the Sun's House colors across their faces. A feather in their hair was to speed them on their way. One of each pair carried sacred meal, the other, pollen. When they met the medicine man who was to be invited with his troupe to dance, they first sprinkled sacred meal on him, and then pollen, to convey the invitation.

In this way the Snake, Ant, Plant, Buffalo, and all other Earth People, as well as all the Thunder and other Sky People, were invited on the fifth day of the ceremony. This was the first and only time the Thunder and Sky People participated in a Fire Dance.

On the sixth day the painting of all the Snake People around the Corn was used in the usual way, i.e., for application to the patients (Newcomb-Reichard, Plate III).

On the seventh day the painting used was that of the Sky-reaching-rock (Newcomb-Reichard, figure 3; *Spider Woman*, p. 194).

The painting of the eighth day was of the House-of-many-points (Plate XIX).

The painting chosen for the last day was the picture of the Skies (see p. 44).

The Fire Dance was held at a place called Black or Lava Rock. The corral was made of lava because of the presence of the Sky People. Nowadays the corral is made of evergreen branches.

Some time after the ceremony for Holy Man and Holy Boy was over, it was decided to have one for Holy Woman and Holy Girl at Mountain-that-fell-out, the home of the Big Snakes. The people made a special *hogan* or medicine lodge in the shape of the horns of the Big Snake.

During the first five days everything was done as in the ceremony for Holy Man and Holy Boy, except that Holy Woman was painted instead of Holy Man, Holy Girl instead of Holy Boy. Otherwise the same paintings were used. In the Shock picture a large white (female) snake had the place of the large black (male) snake in the previous ceremony.

On the sixth day the painting of The Sky People was used.

PLATE XXII. *The Sky People:* The center of the painting indicates its use in the Fire Dance ceremony, as does also its elaboration. The black figure in the center represents the earth surrounded by a corral of yellow pollen and white cornmeal with which the ground is sprinkled before the ceremonial corral is made. The cross in the center represents the large pile of wood, the red cross within it, the fire. The branches around the center stand for two sprigs of oak (at the south and north) and two of blue spruce (at east and west). The real corral may be made of any kind of branches, but ceremonial twigs at least of oak and spruce must be laid in these directions.

Figures of various colors are as follows: at the east, a female and male of the Sky People in black standing on zigzag lightning; at the south, female and male of Sun People in yellow standing on sunbeams; at the west, female and male of Water People in blue standing on flash lightning; and at the north, female and male of Summer People standing on rainbows. A short rainbow lies between each pair and the center.

Each figure is drawn long with dots of contrasting color and black to represent seeds. The collar of otterskin, which features largely in the ceremony, is worn around the neck by each figure, and from it a whistle dangles.

The face of each figure, square for female, round for male, has the white, black, blue and yellow sun streaks symbolical of the Sun's House form of the chant. In addition to the feather bundle representing a waterspout, and the red bonnet with a small turquoise, each figure is provided with horns which represent the crescent moon and the buffalo.

Each female figure carries in its right hand a rattle and a symbol like that which protects its feet, and, suspended on a rain-streamer, Moon's tobacco pouch and the magical traveling hoop. In the left hand each carries a basket and a talking prayerstick. Suspended from the left wrist is a waterjar of the color of the figure to which it belongs.

The males carry the same kinds of objects, but the Sun's tobacco pouch, instead of the Moon's, is suspended from the left hand, making the picture symmetrical in each quarter.

The encircling guardian is the Rainbow; the guardians of the east are white and black Big Flies.

This painting may be used only for the Fire Dance version of the Shooting Chant and is often the first of the four large paintings used.

On the seventh day the people again used the painting of the Sky-reaching-rock (p. 67).
On the eighth day they painted the Home of the Buffalo People (Plate XXIII).
Finally the painting of Earth and Sky was used on the ninth day (p. 45).

These two ceremonies were given to ordain Holy Man, Holy Boy, Holy Woman and Holy Girl in the Shooting Chant. They were told when the Fire Dance should be connected with the ceremony, when to make offerings of sacred meal and when to omit them, and when to ask the Thunder, Hail, Bead or Eagle People to participate.

◇   ◇   ◇

The day after the last ceremony was over Holy Man started out on another hunting trip. He went toward San Francisco Mountains on top of which there is a lake called Crescent lake. From this place he saw what he thought were four mountain sheep. He was afraid of them, remembering his experience on Black Mountain when Thunder captured him. He made a detour of the lake to to get a closer view, but now the animals were on the opposite side. Four times this happened. The fourth time he was able to see that they were buffalo, one black, one white, one blue and one yellow.

Holy Man started to pursue. The buffalo moved on and he followed expecting to get within shooting range. They moved along the Little Colorado (presumably across the mountains near Oraibi. *Interpreter's note*) across Black Mountain and toward Chinlee valley. Holy Man followed. At a point between Chinlee and Round Rock the buffalo stamped on the ground causing a spring of water to flow. They drank from it. They went on between the Lukachukai and Carrizo Mountains to a place called Red Water where they arrived at sunset. All the way, whenever Holy Man stopped to rest, the buffalo also stopped as if they were leading him on.

At Red Water the buffalo waited and showed themselves to Holy Man as Buffalo People. That night Black and Blue Buffalo, the males, gave White and Yellow Buffalo to Holy Man for his mates. They all remained there for the night.

FIGURE 9. *The Buffalo at Red Water:* This picture shows a linear arrangement of the buffalo, a black one at the south, next to it a white one, then a blue, and finally, a yellow buffalo. Each carries a basket made of precious stone, a rattle, and a traveling hoop. All have cloud feet. All are depicted as people wearing the red bonnet of the Shooting Chant. They have the life lines and restoration symbols given to most animals.

A mirage garland encircles three sides of the painting, and a black and a white buffalo guard the east.

Apparently the Buffalo People had heard of Holy Man and these four had been sent to get him so that their prayers and paintings might be included in his powers. They had danced at the Fire Dance at Black Lava Rock, but had not had an opportunity to teach him anything.

The day after Holy Man had lain with the Buffalo women he was ill with fever. He was in a sweat and had a headache. This was because he had not observed the prescribed restriction to remain continent for four days after the ceremony.

Toward dawn one of the buffalo lay down at the east, one at the west, another at the south and the fourth at the north. Wherever they had lain the warmth and perspiration of their bodies made herbs grow. With these they cured Holy Man of his illness, then took him to their home.

As they approached he could see a large pointed white object with a black tip, a black pointed object with white tip, a yellow pointed object tipped with blue, and a blue one tipped with yellow. These were houses of the Buffalo People.

PLATE XXIII. *The Home of the Buffalo People:* One of the most outstanding features of this picture is the symbol of the buffalo houses, the triangular figure shaped like a tipi and set upon a two-colored bar. Since it is doubtful if the buffalo ever came very far into the Navajo territory it is quite appropriate that the legend should take Holy Man into forbidden, *i.e.,* into alien country.

The black center shows the encounter with the Buffalo at Rushing Waters—the great water of the sharp points where lived Water Ox—which Holy Man was forbidden to cross. This water is believed to divide this world from the world beyond. On the black water are four short rainbows signifying protection and purity.

FIGURE 9. THE BUFFALO AT RED WATER

"Because the home of the buffalo is at a place beyond this world, two colors are reversed and white is at the east, black at the north."

The four partial circles which surround the central circle symbolize the supernatural power of the Buffalo over lakes. On each is a dragonfly, the symbol of pure water. It overlaps the outline colors of the black center which for all the circles stand for water, foam, pollen and rainbow as they do in Plates XIII, XXIV. The sacred herbs with curing powers take their roots from the central area which is moist, and white trails always lead the buffalo to pure water.

The white trail leads to the left forefoot of each buffalo. At its right forefoot is the magic hoop which gives power, lightness and speed to anyone possessing it.

The underparts of the buffalo have a yellow outline to represent the warmth and moisture of their bodies which made plants grow and produce pollen.

The peculiar cranklike affair of rain streamer indicates restoration from some calamity, usually death, and is given to many animals (cp. Figures 8, 9).

"The female White Buffalo lives in a house of darkness from the center of which dawn rises (east); the male Black Buffalo lives in a house of dawn from the center of which arises darkness (west); the male Blue Buffalo lives in a sky blue house from the center of which yellow evening light rises up (south); and the female Yellow Buffalo lives in a house of evening light, from the center of which looms blue sky."

This is a quotation from Gray Eye's legend which described the horizontal bars on which the buffalo tipis stand. Miguelito merely says, "The bars are holy."

Instead of the rainbow encircling protector common to many pictures, the buffalo paintings often have a mirage "rope" in all colors. In this picture it is personified. The face and head are represented exactly as are the face and head of other "People" with the turkey-feather bundle which represents a waterspout and the eagle down feather for speed and lightness.

The Buffalo explained that they had brought an Earth Person back with them, and that he had spent the night with the female buffalo. These women were really the wives of the Buffalo-who-never-dies, and their father was the chief of all the Buffalo People. The Buffalo-who-never-dies was the son of the head of the White Buffalo from the far east. The family was angry to hear that Holy Man had taken their women.

They brought food in four baskets, one of jet, one of whiteshell, one of turquoise and a yellow one of abalone. The baskets contained health-giving herbs sprinkled with pollen. After they had eaten, the head of all the Buffalo said, "Now you are in danger. But the people of the earth should know about our powers. What can you do? Can you protect yourself? Do you have any arrows?" Holy Man said he had two, an eagle-feathered arrow and a yellow tail-feathered arrow.

He then made two wands, the feathered wand of mountain mahogany and the red-feathered wand of oak. The Buffalo chief then asked him if he had any sacred soil from Taos (Jemez) Mountain, Mt. Taylor, San Francisco Peaks and La Plata Mountain. Since it is customary for a medicine man to have a small sack containing this soil, he could answer that he had. Then the Buffalo chief said, "You seem to know how to take care of yourself." While the chief was talking to him Holy Man could hear his mother-in-law speaking, although he had never seen her. (This last remark is gratuitous and I am sure Miguelito interpolated it, as was his custom, to turn a joke. Both joke and remark are highly characteristic of Navajo custom. *Author's note.*)

Holy Man made four mountains using some of the soil from each sacred mountain, and named them. He started to arrange them in a row, but the Buffalo Chief said, "If you make them that way the Buffalo-who-never-dies will demolish them at a single charge." Then he arranged them in the four directions and finished before the sun set.

The night was longer than usual, so long that Holy Man called for the dawn. The sun finally appeared but instead of the usual white light, in the east there was a red glare which shone over Rushing Water. This red light indicated danger. Just after the sun rose Buffalo-who-never-dies charged in a mighty rush which took him across Rushing Water toward the house of the Buffalo Chief where he asked for Holy Man.

When the Buffalo People saw him coming they all wailed and shouted, and Holy Man took his two wives to the top of Jemez Mountain. The angry Buffalo discovered them there and charged, rushing past the mountain in a half circle, and returning, rushed at it from the east demolishing that side. Holy Man and his wives stood on a sunbeam as he shot at the charging Buffalo with the eagle-feathered arrow. The arrow went home but did not kill. The sunbeam carried the party to the mountain of the west, San Francisco Peaks. The Buffalo-who-never-dies charged and demolished the west side of the mountain, and Holy Man shot him with the feathered wand. The sunbeam carried the hunter to Mt. Taylor, the mountain of the south, where once more the Buffalo charged. This time he was shot with the yellow tail-feathered arrow. The sunbeam moved with its party to the mountain of the north, La Plata. As the Buffalo-who-never-dies charged from the north, he rushed so hard that he missed La Plata Mountain, and Holy Man, hitting him with the red-feathered wand, finally killed him.

Since this animal embodied the life of all the Buffalo People, all buffalo died with him except the women Holy Man had taken for his wives. When he realized this, Holy Man sat down on a rock and bowed his head with remorse as his bow lay lifeless on his knees. The older Buffalo woman sat down on one side of him, put her arm around his shoulder and said, "Now what can we do? You have killed all our relatives."

On the other side the younger, embracing him, said, "Since you have so many powers, even power to kill, you must also have power to bring them back to life." He replied that he had.

Then he told the women to turn their backs and not under any circumstances to turn their heads, for if they did so, his powers would fail. They obeyed and he went to his victim and pulled out the weapons, one by one: the eagle-feathered arrow, the feathered wand, the yellow tail-feathered arrow and the red-feathered wand. As he did so he rubbed dust from his own moccasins first on one side of the buffalo, then on the other, then on its head, and all the while he prayed.

When Holy Man had finished the last prayer Buffalo-who-never-dies came to life. He rose and said, "Your power is greater than mine. I give up and you may have the two women."

Holy Man told him how to bring the other buffalo to life saying that each in turn should restore the next one. They did this and all were restored save one, for one of the wives disobeyed and turned her head for just a moment. The Black Buffalo accounted for all their numbers, as did the White and the Blue Buffalo, but the Yellow Buffalo missed one and found him lying dead.

Holy Man told them that there were four old Turkey Buzzards who could bring him to life. They made offerings of valuable skins and precious stones to the Turkey Buzzards, but they refused to help. Then Big Fly whispered that they should withdraw these offerings and give just a little carrion. They tried that and the Turkey Buzzards performed a ceremony which brought the Yellow Buffalo to life.

Shortly after this occurrence all the buffalo started on a journey to the east and Holy Man went with them. They crossed the red river and camped on the other side. The second night they crossed Wide Water and camped for the night. The third day they crossed where there is a stone bridge at the junction of two rivers, and spent a night. The next day they came to the Waters-rushing-in-opposite-directions and the buffalo crossed. Holy Man was just about to cross when Talking God appeared before him and said, "You must not attempt to cross because the dangers on the other side are beyond your powers. The waters are inhabited by the Water Oxen and they might devour you. But even if you should succeed in crossing, you would never return, never would you see your father, or mother, or brothers and sisters again."

Although Holy Man did not heed the warnings of most people he met, he listened to Talking God and returned to Whirling Mountain. When he got back he and Holy Boy discussed in the greatest detail every item of their unusual and protracted experiences. The question of healing herbs concerned them especially and they decided to return to the scene of Holy Boy's adventures on Mt. Taylor. As they talked all the way, the distance seemed short and before they realized it they had arrived at the home of the Ant People who had given Holy Boy the medicines. He had never paid for it, and as they approached, the Ant People derided him saying, "Here come Holy Man and Holy Boy again. They never paid us for the medicine we gave them when they were here before." They seemed very angry and shot both of the visitors twice, then took them captive and started east with them in the direction taken by the buffalo.

[71]

They first crossed a river of pure water where Holy Man and Holy Boy partially revived. Before they reached the red river Talking God appeared again and warned them not to go on. He said they should pay the Ant People buckskins which had been taken from unwounded deer and treated in ceremonial fashion. They did this and the Ant People released them.

Talking God then proposed that they hurry back to Whirling Mountain and have a ceremony. Coyote said, "We should not be in a hurry. Let us take four days. That will give us time to collect plants and cure the wounds of Holy Man and Holy Boy. We should also send word and get two Earth People to learn the paintings and rites so they may be useful to Earth People." This coyote was from the home of Monster Slayer at the Place-of-emergence. When they reached their home at Whirling Mountain two runners, who were as fast as the wind, were there before them. They were called Youth-who-runs-like-a-white-streak and One-who-looks-backward.

At the end of the four days all the Earth People once more assembled. Holy Man and Holy Boy told the story of all their experiences on earth and in the sky. They taught their lore—paintings, rites, medicines, prayers and songs—to Youth-who-runs-like-a-white-streak and One-who-looks-backward in the order in which they had learned them. The people who were not human—snakes, thunders, buffalo and all other animals—were there, and after the two youths had mastered the instructions it was decreed that these people should never speak on earth again. The original paintings were taken back to the sky. They had been painted on skin, clouds and other perishable materials. One reason they were transferred to man's memory was to keep people from quarreling over them as material possessions. Another reason was that they would thus survive as long as man was interested enough to apply himself to learning them. The clouds and skins given by the sky people were perishable and would wear out. Since that time paintings have been made in sand and have been obliterated every time they have been used.

Before the conclusion of the final ceremony Holy Man said, "There is still one thing lacking, the painting of the Buffalo People." He went to the place where he had killed the Buffalo-who-never-dies and returned at midnight with the painting.

PLATE XXIV. *The Buffalo-who-never-dies:* This picture depicts the restoration of the Buffalo-who-never-dies. Except that the colors are changed, the center looks the same as that of Plate XXIII. In this case the black center is a lake with reflected rainbows, and on each side of it are the four mountains which Holy Man built to cope with the Buffalo. The horizontal bars indicating the sky colors of the buffalo homes are next to the mountains, and the short rainbows lie above.

The herbs are those which brought the Buffalo-who-never-dies back to life.

At the east Holy Boy is shown pulling the eagle-feathered arrow out of the black buffalo which has the characteristic white trail leading off from one front foot, the traveling hoop held in the other, the underpart coated with pollen, the symbol of restoration on the back.

Holy Boy is dressed and accoutered as usual and wears the red bonnet. He carries the black bow in his left hand as usual, but the eagle-feathered arrow is in the buffalo instead of in his right hand. He carries in his right hand therefore the buffalo hide rattle which aided him in his songs for restoration.

At the south Holy Boy stands, distinguished from Holy Man only by the yellow-feathered arrow in the blue buffalo.

Holy Woman with the vari-colored tapered body, the eagle-feathered wand (in the white buffalo), and the yellow bow stands at the west. Her counterpart, Holy Girl, is at the north, her red-feathered wand in the yellow buffalo.

Another painting in the collection, somewhat simpler than this, since it does not have the plants at the corners, has the following explanation of the same center: "The black represents the motion of the mountains; the white, the motion of the rocks; the blue, the motion of the clouds; the yellow, the motion of the waters."

This symbolism is doubtless not different from that of Plate XXIV, but only a ritualistic or supernatural (*i.e.* poetic) symbolism in addition to the naturalistic.

A number of the Buffalo People came back with Holy Man. They then arranged all the song groups of the Shooting Chant and decreed how the songs should be used in connection with the paintings, rites and prayers. They then sang all the songs belonging to the various ceremonies by way of review. Holy Man told Earth People that if they ever needed him they should make his painting, and pray to him at Whirling Mountain. He also taught them the paintings of Monster Slayer, giving them the one of the Four Mountains, the House-of-many-points, and the House-of-moving-points. He told them that by using these they could get help from Monster Slayer, the great War god.

Holy Man also explained that he and Holy Boy would take back to the skies with them the sacred paraphernalia which they had brought to teach the people: the baskets of precious stones, the arrows of turquoise, whiteshell, abalone and redstone. They told the people to use ordinary baskets instead, and to make arrows of reed and other plants. They were to fasten to them beads of the representative stones to indicate their divine origin. They said the reason for this was that the original articles could not be replaced, repaired or duplicated, whereas the symbols of the originals made of earthy materials could be secured and made by all those who learned the chant, and would thus be available to all the Earth People who needed them.

Holy Man and Holy Boy remained one day and one night after the end of the final ceremony. Just at dawn of the second day they embraced their animal relatives, once more telling the Ant, Spider, Snake, Buffalo and other People to represent them here on the earth. They said they would be living in the sky where the same places existed with the same names as those on the earth. They said they would never meet again on earth but would meet again in another world. Holy Man and Holy Boy spoke thus for the last time.

Then Holy Man, Holy Boy, Holy Woman, Holy Girl, Monster Slayer, Child-of-the-water, Reared-within-the-earth, Changing Grandchild, Talking God, *xactčé'óɣan* and all of the other Holy Ones vanished. They arose into the sky and were seen no more.

VIII

Artistry of Legend and Sandpainting

Navajo art, like the art of most primitive peoples, has interest and charm because of the originality of its viewpoint. Taking all knowledge for its field, uncircumscribed by space, and with all the facilities of which imagination is capable, the myths and their tangible representation in plastic forms are all-embracing. There are certain general principles upon which the word- and sand-pictures are based, but it is from the selection and variation of details, many of which are daring, that the art gains its unusual character.

The physician or nurse can see in the Navajo chant only something to be stamped out. In identifying himself with deity and communicating divine power to the patient, the chanter may rub tallow, ceremonially prepared, over his own eyes and then over the eyes of the patient, and do other similar things. If he happens to have trachoma the identification must nevertheless be made, for the "god of the germ" is unknown. But if the chant can be looked at from the viewpoint of the meaning explained in its legend, it is found to be a work of art. The very premises of the religion afford unlimited scope. Space is defined as unbounded; there is earth, sky, a land "beyond the sky," a world under the earth. Time, as we have seen, is also without definiteness, but the significant incidents of any particular span of time function as potently today or fifty years hence as they did in legendary times "before the world was like it is now." For this reason, if such an incident is repeated, it has power as strong as the day it was first enacted.

Within the realms of sky, earth and subterranean worlds there are people who properly belong in one realm or another. Their offices are not exclusive, however, and it is better to have coöperation amongst them. Birds are earthly beings in a sense, but they travel spaces to which man can aspire only in his mind. They are therefore connecting links between earth and sky. Sometimes snakes are thought of as governing the regions underground, but in the Bead Chant they are provided with feathers, so that their power of swift darting, added to the power of the large birds' flight, enables them to lift a heavy earth person through the sky.

Thunders are "sky people" whose essential concern is moisture, rainfall, water. Waters on the earth, and deep waters, as well as subterranean currents, are also controlled. The water ox which has many features in common with thunder and is believed to have similar powers, indicates the relationship between the sky and deep waters. Birds and earth people are tangibles; sky, thunders and water monsters are visualized through Navajo imagination. The dawn, blue sky, yellow evening light and night are conceived as somewhat birdlike for they "fly," their means of flight being wings or feathers. These feathers may actually be visualized, as they are in Figure 2, (c) and (d), or more remote symbols may be used for them. The long stiff eagle feathers of Talking God symbolize the first rays of dawn (Plate XX), the "feathers" upon which it travels. Here is a combination of a natural phenomenon with the motivating force of a bird and the personal characteristics of an idealized man. Carrying the unification a little further, the Navajo represent lifelike birds as heralds of the skies.

It is quite possible that Navajo belief does not accept power unless it be exceptional. Man has powers of his own, but in Navajo thought these alone cannot suffice for his earthly struggle. He must attract to himself the powers of other beings. And similarly, other beings must combine their own powers with those of other kinds. Wolf, Mountain Lion, Wildcat, Bobcat and Badger are hunters *par excellence* and their hunting powers are respected and sought, but in addition to control over flesh food, Navajo dogma gives them also magical power over corn which stands for all vegetation (Plates V, VI, VII). In the same way, and for reasons not obvious, snakes of all kinds have power over game, as is evidenced by the chevron marked on their bodies. They also have control over corn or vegetable food, as well as over healing herbs (Plates XIV, XV, XVI).

We as white people frequently congratulate ourselves on the range of our abstract ideas. So admirable do we sometimes find them as to assert that abstract ideas are impossible to primitive peoples. A Navajo might well ask a professor of philosophy how the dawn looks, and finding that professor unable to picture the dawn either verbally or plastically might scornfully contend that the white man's idea of the dawn had not been worked out to its ultimate conclusion. The Navajo has an abstraction of the different skies, and he has gone beyond the abstraction to make it tangible to the man on the trail. This he has done repeatedly in the symbols of his paintings, several of the most striking of which are the representations of blue necks with four red stripes as ''life,'' and of rainbows on the grinding stone of Plate XV as ''power of the hands.''

Another example is that of the ''suns,'' that is, the group including Sun, Moon, and Black and Yellow Winds. They have additional power in horns which correspond to the feathers or wings of the skies. They have eyes and mouths like persons, but they are also represented as being carried in baskets ornamented with feathers (Figure 4). Such visualization is not only realistic and artistic, but it is ritualistic as well, for no sacred object should be placed on the ground, but should be kept in a basket which is thought of as made of precious stones.

The dogma which demands that every realm of knowledge or imagination shall partake of characteristics of every other reminds one strongly of the harmony between jewels, birds, flowers, animals, natural phenomena and man in certain Mexican religions. In some measure, with different stresses, Navajo religion and art show a modification of such ideas which no doubt are related. It does not seem likely that the Navajo got their religious ideas directly from the Aztecs, but persistent study of Navajo culture shows that its differences in symbolism and emphasis must have reached them indirectly through various other peoples, such as the Pueblos and certain Plains tribes. The Navajo are adaptable people who do not view ideas in exactly the same way as their originators, and Navajo religion must be regarded as representing constant growth and reinterpretation of ideas they may have brought with them, combined with those which they have taken over from others, and once more revamped.

Their adaptability is clearly manifested in the field which concerns this work. The pueblo Indians have altars with many fragile and bulky properties which presuppose possibilities of storage between rituals. The nomadic life of the Navajo prevents them from caring for bulky altarpieces of stone, pottery and wood. They can, however, and do, represent many of the same things in sand. Indeed, they may upon occasion symbolize in sand even those altar parts which they ordinarily might make more permanent. The chanter of the nine-night Sun's House ritual of the Male Shooting Chant should have a booth which is the symbol of the Sun's House, but lacking it, need not hesitate to sing the chant in this wise, since he may have the Sun's House picture made in sand (Figure 1). He should collect feathers or send for evergreen branches for other rites, but failing success in obtaining these objects, symbols of them may be strewn in sand and are considered effective. The Navajo believes that things are what one says they are.

Navajo mythology demonstrates, if nothing else did, the numerous sources to which the culture is indebted. There is a large body of mythological episodes peculiar to the American continent. The story of the adventures of the boy (often twin) heroes, built up as are those of the

Shooting Chant, is an example. Holy Man and Holy Boy, who represent Monster Slayer and Child-of-the-water, pursue their quest, and submit to tests by fire, smoking, and freezing in a manner that is American Indian as contrasted to plot development of the Old World. That which makes the incidents unique to the Navajo is the clever way in which the incidents are strung together to form a well-developed plot, and the way in which every act is made to have ceremonial significance. All things have a purpose, and the purpose of an escapade, which in many tribes might be of only literary or social significance, is to the Navajo in a chant myth religious or ritualistic.

A number of chant legends are now available and all show approximately the same construction. People are having a hard time to secure subsistence, or have some grievance. A boy of the family is forbidden to go somewhere or to do some particular thing. He does not observe the warning and does that which was forbidden, whereupon he embarks upon a series of adventures which keep him away from home so long that his family despairs of his return. Many of the adventures incorporate episodes common to American mythology, but in the chant lore of the Navajo each nets the hero some item which will in future be important in the chant. The tests given his children by the Sun—smoking, freezing, sweating—are examples. The Visit to the Sun had many useful results, not the least of which was the acquisition of the sacred arrows which are the chief symbol of the Shooting Chant. Each sandpainting is another example. The stress in each case is on the eradication of ignorance by substituting instruction.

After the dramatic episodes, the hero returns to his home bringing with him the ritualistic lore which he teaches to his brother. He has been away so long and has become so accustomed to association with deity that his own people seem impure to him. He corrects that fault by teaching them the means of purification. This part of the myth often goes over into minute descriptions of ceremonial details. The hero is completely engrossed in ritual, and after teaching it to his brother, he repeats it by having his brother sing over his sister so as to rehearse under the hero's directions. Earth ways eventually become boring to the one who has become accustomed to adventure, and he finally bids his family goodbye, saying they will never see him again but he will always be with them in spirit. He then vanishes into the air, presumably to join the gods whom he has come to resemble.

All bodies of mythology have style which is built up by selection of plot, episodes, characters and figures of speech from the infinite number of possible details. Hawaiian mythology constantly uses color, natural phenomena and symbolic metaphors to gain its effect, which is largely religious, but seeks also to honor chieftainship. The outstanding feature of Pawnee mythology is a preoccupation with stars, and that of certain Salish Indians of the North, an interest in sound, while at the same time they neglect color, stars and other natural phenomena.

Navajo mythology, like the Hawaiian, dwells upon natural phenomena, but in a way which gives it quite a different character. The Hawaiian is concerned with clouds, mists, mountains, volcanoes and with color as it compares with material earthly objects. The Navajo has certain set patterns of imagery like the sky colors, the rainbow, zigzag and flash lightnings, sunbeams, rain streamers, cloud blankets or curtains of various colors. Red is the color of danger, and by the Navajo logic, protection from danger. Direction—east, south, west, north, always mentioned either in a sunwise circuit or east-west, south-north in a cross—is also important and gives opportunity for fourfold repetition. Up to the zenith may often be added, making five also a literary, as well as a ritualistic, pattern of repetition.

It is impossible to determine whether ritualistic grew out of artistic devices or the reverse. It is more than likely that they grew up together, influencing one another reciprocally. Navajo art by no means restricts itself to the use of four and five, but they are the most common numbers according-to-holiness, and repetition in the form of multiples, twelve, twenty-four and forty-eight, adds power religiously, and beauty artistically, in Navajo speculation. So important is the number four that characters of the legends give a false or noncommittal answer three times, but are compelled to answer, and to answer truthfully, the fourth time. This device is illustrated by Holy Man and Holy Boy who, in answer to the Sun's question, ''Are you warm?'' answered, ''No,'' three times during the sweating test. The fourth time they answered truthfully, ''Yes.'' Three times Holy Man said he had no tobacco when he was asked for it by Big Snake Man, but the fourth time produced a pouch containing two kinds.

The Scavenger of the Bead Chant worked six days for the inhabitants of White House and five for those of Blue House, and it was on the twelfth day after his arrival that his life changed. Twenty-four ''eagles,'' meaning eagles and hawks, assisted at conveying Scavenger to the sky in some versions, but if the chanter has sufficient help in making the sandpainting, forty-eight is a better number. Number is as important artistically as ritualistically in myth and painting.

Indeed it is impossible to separate art and ritual. Many of the ritualistic arts are aesthetic. The whole fabrication of prayersticks and bundle paraphernalia is an aesthetic occupation, felt as such by the men who pursue it. The materials, reeds, paints, tiny pieces of the precious stones, feathers of bright-plumaged birds, pollen, the crystal with which the sun's power is brought to them—all of these things are handled, not only with reverence by the men, but also with pleasure expressed verbally as they work. The same kind of satisfaction is shown in the achievement represented by a sandpainting. The presentation of an offering by laying it on the feet of a supernatural being, his taking it up by running it along the two sides of his body, and his acceptance of it by breathing in from it, are ritualistic acts as beautiful as they are sacred. From many points of view the transformation of the eagle feather into a wolf, of a yellow hawk feather into a mountain lion, of the blue hawk feather into a beaver and of a magpie feather into an otter (p. 32), is an episode more poetic than religious. This incident illustrates also the close relationship felt by the Navajo between birds, prey animals and water animals, and it signifies the stress on life, for these changes brought about the restoration of Scavenger who had been destroyed by Coyote.

An outstanding characteristic of American mythology in general, and of Navajo mythology in particular, is a genius for characterization. It is so apparent in the myths of this work that only a few examples will suffice. The Sun, most powerful of the supernaturals, is represented as husband, lover, philanderer, a cruel father who later becomes kind, as a vulnerable human who weeps when his sons make an unusual request, as one susceptible to the tantrums of his sky wife, as one generous with one side of his heart and with the other sufficiently repentant of his generosity to withhold from earth people his most cherished possessions, the arrows of precious stones. On the other hand, he is respectful of, as well as amused by, their daring, when his sons irreverently challenge him to swallow the sacred arrows, and upon his refusal, demonstrate their own powers by doing so.

Still another choice bit is in the imagery of the Sun's tobacco pouch which is worked out in the finest detail. The pouch made of skin dyed red is represented as embroidered with porcupine quills. The blue disk on it is the Sun himself; the blue triangle is the pipe, cylindrical as is the sacred pipe belonging to the chant. At the stem is a black dot representing a bit of tobacco, and at the bowl a white streak which stands for a smoke. And, as if these were not sufficient to indicate human needs and pleasures, there is sometimes a blue line beside the pipe and running its entire length which represents the Sun's pipe-cleaner!

The wife of the Sun who lives with him in the sky is represented as very worldly. She guards his household, protects the children from his wrath, and at the same time chides him with unfaithfulness as the fact of his children proves. Before the Sun accepts the children as his own, she, womanlike, defends them, but later demands her own proof of their inheritance when she asks them to cure her own son who has been bitten by a watersnake.

Navajo myth, as well as plastic art, exploits the use of contrast, and Changing Woman is so perfect that she is a foil to the Sun's wife with whom he lives. She never goes into a rage although she sometimes expresses fear. Her equanimity and modesty as the mother of the wonderful warrior twins are always outstanding. And yet the Sun and those very twins found her adamant against moving from her home, where living was uncomfortable and subsistence hard to find, to the new flint-protected home they had made for her in the west. She was afraid she would be lonesome without all her acquaintances and friends, and they had to promise her companionship and frequent visits, all reactions which are strictly human and which the Navajo stress.

Another frequently used device, amply illustrated by the myths we have here, is the contrast between the insignificant and the importance of its power. Scavenger, whose very name indicates his inferiority, is really a great hero in disguise, and the story of the Bead Chant is the Navajo version of the "poor boy who made good." His name is purposely used to contrast with his power and the reverence which the modest should rightly inspire. Holy Man and Holy Boy stemmed from a humble origin but early in the story demonstrate the noble side of their birth. Cedar waxwing is a still better example, for all he had to offer was a string of five flint knives, but without it Holy Boy could not subsequently have released himself from the maw of the giant fish. Another small bird modestly contributed two songs to the power of the boys (p. 38), and others simply gave names of dangerous animals, or warnings. Yet if any one of these small gifts had been lacking, the trip to the Sun would have failed, for each was important in the success of the venture, and each is duly appreciated by the Navajo so as to be represented in the chant.

Another evidence of the use of contrast is the necessity of pairing. One indispensable element of this notion is the confirmed Navajo belief that neither sex is self-sufficient, but both are necessary to fulfilment of any sort. This notion is an obvious one and common to many tribes, but the Navajo carry it further. There are many cases where two beings of the same kind are paired, yet they are both males or females. Holy Man (Monster Slayer) and Holy Boy (Child-of-the-water); Sun and Moon; Talking God and xactčé'óɣan; Changing Woman and Salt Woman who lived together; and Holy Woman and Holy Girl are pairs of this kind. These combinations seem to point to the emphasis that weaker, more gentle powers are as necessary to well-being as the stronger more forceful ones. This explanation is a religious one in the light of the Navajo effort to secure harmony, but it seems also to be an artistic one necessary in securing balance, symmetry, and contrast.

Instead of the interpretation "male" and "female" which for a long time has been prevalent, I think the contrast "strong, forceful, dominating" not as opposed to, but rather as complementary to, "weak, submissive," more accurate. The blue Sun is paired with the white Moon, but calls him "uncle." Blue and black are "male," or better "dominating" colors in the Shooting Chant, white and yellow are the "female" or "submissive" colors, but white is the ordinary contrast to black, and yellow to blue. In representing the sun-group, however, white (Moon) goes with blue (Sun), yellow with black (Winds). Holy Man usually takes the lead, telling Holy Boy what to do. Holy Boy expects to be told, has the attitude of obedience to his older brother's commands, occasionally takes the lead when success depends upon quiet effort. In the introduction of the Shooting Chant myth Changing Woman is said to live with Salt Woman, but in other tales she is said to live with her sister, Whiteshell Woman, at the home in the west. It is difficult to get at the function of Whiteshell Woman and I believe she exists simply because of the literary device which exploits pairing and contrast.

Some of these examples have demonstrated another element of style, the use of humor, for contrary to general opinion, Indians have a fine appreciation of humor although it may differ in many respects from our own. The Navajo enjoys all the implications in depicting the jealous wife. The injection of the statement made by Miguelito that Holy Man could hear, but could not see, his buffalo mother-in-law, is definitely humorous, for even though the Navajo observe mother-in-law avoidance quite seriously, they have as many mother-in-law jokes as we have. But the joke takes a social rather than a personal turn, and they ridicule the peculiar custom rather than the individual. Although the feathers shed by the young eagles on the enemies of Scavenger represent a punishment which led to serious results, the Navajo is not above enjoying the spectacle of all the pueblo people afflicted with an itching disease. Besides the humor of situation, they also enjoy the satisfaction of poetic justice which is a major point in the plot of the Bead Chant.

The body of mythology of most primitive people is often the source of ethical authority. Ethics and morals differ so greatly among various tribes that it is often impossible to distinguish sharply between morals and ethics, and etiquette. It has already been indicated that a wrong, evil or sin to the Navajo means being out of the natural order. They have no notion of future punishment dependent upon man's life in this world, and it is not difficult to understand why they have never accepted the devil or hell of Christian theology. Sin to them is error, breaking the law. The way to correct it is to become informed, to take measures to get back into the stride of tradition. Usually this can be done by ritual, and in any case, it is fatalistic. Man may do all he can to make his way consonant with that of tribal teachings, but if ritual fails, then all has failed. As an individual there is nothing he can do about it.

The myths of our two chants demonstrate the attitude. Various beings, Arrow Man, Big Thunder and Buffalo, are said to have sent for Holy Man, because they were angry at him, but when he arrived they told him that he had erred through ignorance, and the whole burden of his audience with them was instruction (pp. 57, 60, 70) in which anger was dissolved. One might even say that perfect knowledge and understanding is the panacea for the ills of man. Such understanding can be achieved only by insinuating oneself into the mind and thought of an unlimited number of supernatural beings and becoming like them.

Customs which with us might have more to do with manners than with morals are reflected in the myth style. One which comes out more clearly in the Navajo text than in translation of Miguelito's narrative is the use of terms of address. A Navajo is exceedingly rude, in fact, he may even be thought to hold a grudge, if he does not use a term of address even to a stranger. The term he uses is never the name of the person, but rather a kin-term. There are many examples in the legends to show that the use of the name indicates power over the one to whom it belongs. If a Navajo meets an absolute stranger, he may address him as "my friend," but it may not be long before he uses a more intimate term such as "my grandfather (grandchild)," "my brother," or if the circumstances permit greater familiarity, "my son-in-law." Throughout the texts strangers into whose domain Holy Man and Holy Boy intrude address them as, "my daughter's child, my son's child," for since the strangers do not know the boys, they consider it best to use both terms of respect until they find out which is correct.

It is only a matter of decent upbringing for a Navajo to state the name of the place which he calls home and the clan to which he belongs, as soon as he enters the camp of a stranger. Until he does this he is under suspicion. Someone may even say, "What is this person?" instead of "Who is this person?" For this reason it was a reprimand to Holy Boy, a warning to mind his manners, when the chief of the Ants said to him, "It is only proper to tell where you are from (p. 61)". Myths constantly reflect the customs of the Navajo, the more so the closer the translation is to the language in which they are conceived.

Many of the principles which determine the literary style operate also for the paintings, but of course there is greater freedom of word than there is in plastic composition. Most pictures, for instance, are arranged symmetrically or in divisions of four, and generally, grouping in fives is left for subordinating details—bunches of feathers on the rainbow, arrows or lightnings on head or in hand, packs on the backs of the badgers of Plate VII. In the stories, where there is greater freedom, five is a common number in description, as it is also in the verses of the songs and prayers. The only pictures where five has reference to the major figures are Plates V, VI, VII of the Bead Chant where five hunting animals are represented on each side of a center.

Three forms of pictorial composition are most common, although they are by no means the only ones. The simplest of these is a linear arrangement of similar figures (Plates X, XI, XX, Figure 9). Sometimes there is a row of figures placed in mirror symmetry (Plates II-VII). The third, and perhaps most favored, arrangement is with figures placed in the quadrants formed by the four directions so as to form a St. Andrew's cross. Frequently some element, like a plant, snake, or buffalo, is used to mark off the quarters, such elements forming a Maltese cross. All the elements in this arrangement are placed around a center which is as important ritualistically as it is aesthetically. The center explains the setting of the scene to him who knows, it unifies the composition for him who only sees and who does not understand. By variation on the centers very striking effects are achieved (Plates XVII, XVIII, XIX).

Centers demonstrate another principle of composition which holds throughout, namely, the disregard for perspective. The center of Plate XIII, by the presence of the ladder, represents the place where the Navajo emerged, the ladder showing the relationship of this to the lower world and the need of the people for a means of egress. It further represents the home of the Arrow People, as shown by the locust and grebe placed outside the circle. We are constantly impressed by the lack of perspective, its place being taken by symbolism and understanding of that symbolism.

Where there is great freedom of symbolic representation there is often lack of artistic unity, but that is not the case with most Navajo pictures since the desire for harmony integrates all symbolic details. Black Thunder has blue wing tips to show the protection of his mate, Blue Thunder, and Blue Thunder has black wing tips for the same reason. This principle, carried out consistently, makes for contrast, variety and balance, all principles of fundamental artistic importance.

Unity is secured also by the so-called "rope," or encircling guardian, which encompasses three sides of most pictures. The east side is left open, a ritualistic requirement which prevents the "spirit of the picture (and of those who make and use it) from being bound in." But it is also an aesthetic device, for it prevents monotony and gives the picture motion which it might otherwise lack.

Scavenger in the Eagle's Nest (Plate I) is a rare exception to the law of unity which, even without perspective, is so outstanding. The interest in this picture is of a different nature, since it stresses the details of the story. The relationship between boy, basket, and food animals is not very apparent, and the absence of guardians leaves the elements of the picture with a somewhat scattered effect. Looked at from another point of view the picture falls into a known, but not common, class of Navajo paintings which depicts the action almost entirely in the enlarged center (cp. Newcomb-Reichard, Plate XV).

One detail of arrangement is subtle and typically Navajo. That is the placing of the boy's head over the colored bounding lines of the blue center which stands for the eagle's nest. It is impossible to tell whether this arrangement is used to relate the boy to the world outside the nest, or for artistic reasons. It is likely that both reasons function.

The position of the dragonflies of Plates XXIII, XXIV shows that the arrangement is not accidental, but one common to the Navajo style. The only place in which I know of it elsewhere is on the designs of the extinct pottery of the Mimbres Valley.

The paintings of the Bead Chant are unusual in several ways, another being that in none of the paintings we have is the center with cross or two-cross arrangement used. I do not know whether this is accidental, ritualistic, or due to the fact that there may be other paintings which we have not found.

Something has already been said about symmetrical arrangement. Perhaps more usual than mirror symmetry (as in Plates V, VI, VII, XXII) is the rhythmic repetition of similar figures around a central axis (Figures 4, 5) in which the main and subsidiary figures are placed in the same position, thus giving the picture the effect of lively motion. Motion is somewhat more common than mirror symmetry in Navajo sandpaintings. But, with the Navajo talent for balance, formalized by the desire to prevent "overdoing," the pictures never involve the spectator in a labyrinthine motion with them. Plate XXIII, The Home of the Buffalo People, is an excellent illustration of this fact. With just a little less restraint the white trails which lead from the feet of the buffalo to water might hopelessly include the onlooker. As it is, the eye moves along the graceful curves just far enough for enjoyment, not so far as to become confused. The austere lines of the tipilike homes, the curves of the lakes where the trails end and the encircling mirage guardian, all contribute to pleasing limitation.

The Shock Painting (Plate XXI) is an example of a picture constructed according to compositional principles quite different from those mentioned, and unlike that of Scavenger in the Eagle's Nest, perfectly unified. The tracks lead the eye, as the verbal explanation suggests, right into the picture which, though simple, is effective.

The use of color, with careful consideration of values, is another factor in the achievement of symmetry, balance and unity. Pairing of colors, previously mentioned, with the addition of red, is one method. Outlining with the four colors not in the body of the design makes for unity. It should be noticed that red, being one of the dark colors, is used at such portions of the picture as to make it a bounding color, even as is black in this art and many others with which we are familiar. The ceremonial explanation of the position of red is that it surrounds because it warns of, or protects from, danger. The aesthetic reason that it unifies is not mentioned, but is doubtless felt.

The exaggeration of red reaches its peak in the idea behind it, as well as in the portrayal of the scene of Plate XVI. This picture is essentially the same as that of Plate XIV, but the use of red brings out startling effects quite different from any others. A black snake is outlined in white. When red takes the place of black and the white outline is retained, the figure becomes something quite new. The same is true when the black figures outlined in white become red. The use of red is carried out consistently, and the picture is one of many examples which cause astonishment because of the tremendous difference in effect caused by only a slight change in technique.

There are cases where ritualistic requirements prevent the fullest expression of the artistic principle of regular repetition. Just as every chant has positive requirements, so also has it taboos. It was ordained that no snakes should take part in the Hail Chant, and that watersnake should never enter into the affairs of the Shooting Chant. Consequently there are only three kinds of snakes pictured in the Shooting Chant, and since there are four positions in the cross-arrangement, Big Snakes are used at east and west, whereas Crooked Snakes are placed at the south and Arrowsnakes at the north. Aesthetic demands which match other subjects could have used four kinds of snakes very nicely.

The artistic devices of the Navajo are few and simple, and although the whole culture shows rich enjoyment in repetition, the pictures give evidence of great variety. The reason for this is the unexpected twist which furnishes surprise. After seeing a very large number of pictures depicting snakes, I came to the conclusion that there *could* be no more possibilities for snake arrangements, and yet every new picture I see of the Wind Chant offers an arrangement as unexpected as it is original. However disconnected Plate I may seem, it has numerous points of interest, especially after the details are understood. The conception of snakes with bird-power on the shoulders, and as encircling guardians (Plate III) is another surprise. The composition of Big Thunder (frontispiece) is so unusual as to be spectacular, and yet the utilization of the main theme for background with the smaller repetitions of the same motive superimposed upon it is a simple enough treatment.

Sandpaintings, like all other products of primitive art, are always individual. One may say that no two are alike if one makes allowance for tradition which demands similarity for pictures of the same title, and even in those, slight variations may be seen due to styles of individual medicine men. Conscious variation, which may make a picture "entirely different" in the minds of the chanters, is achieved by variation in the position or shape of details as much as by change in composition. For this reason such series of paintings as those of the Arrow People (Plates XI, XII, XIII), of the Snakes (Plates XIV, XV, XVI), and those of the heroes armored in flint (Plates X, XVII, XVIII, XIX), have been selected for illustration. The differences are quite obvious, some depending on color which shows up in the colored plates, others being changes of composition which the drawings demonstrate.

In considering the myths and the paintings of the Navajo one wonders—without arriving at a satisfactory conclusion—what gave rise to the selection of details which are used. For, just as the small birds had a major part in the great adventure of the Holy Ones, so also the carefully selected, planned and executed details make for the beauty and subtlety of the art. The small elements which go to make up the Sun's tobacco pouch; representation of a home with smokehole and fire; or of corral, woodpile and fire of the Fire Dance; the shaping of the Arrow People with arrow bodies and outspread arms forming bows; the harmony with which the flint arrowpoints is worked out; providing Thunders with the maximum of storm ideas—rainbows, waterspouts, rain, lightnings—all of these are vivid illustrations of the fertility of the Navajo mind. The charm with which "people" are impressionistically represented by gay little heads which peer out over the background is as indescribable as it is surprising. This is done for Sky People in Figure 1, for Medicine People in Figure 3, for Snake People in Plate XV. In paintings of the Hail and Wind Chants, Cactus People are shown with little faces growing from the branching stems. Similarly attractive is the representation of thunder's reverberation as a curved feather at the sides of the tail.

The details of the composition of Scavenger in the Eagle's Nest (Plate I) are interesting in that they provide for all human requirements. There seems to be no reason why the boy should not be carried in a dark cloud, but he needs a crystal for a flashlight, a whistle for ventilation. And although on the first day he can eat the leftovers of the eaglets' meal raw, after the return of the parent eagles, he must have not only the best of man-made food, and the purest of water, but they must be served in a pottery bowl and reed tubes.

There is no possibility of predicting what details will be selected, and just as surprising as those used is the omission of others. The Navajo are always preoccupied with the water supply, as is demonstrated by Plate I. Nevertheless there is no spring in the painting of the Home of the Eagles (Plate IV), although in the legend it is supposed to lie within the plaza around which these pueblolike dwellings are built.

Navajo chant legend shares with other American mythologies certain stereotyped but interesting episodes, a talent for characterization and accurate observation, an enjoyment of humor and use of pathos. It is distinguished by the selection of literary devices. Ritualistic demands draw all episodes and details together so that the plot of the whole is unified. Imagery includes personification, extensive use of natural phenomena as persons or as figures of speech, always within the ritualistic rôle. Color is extensively used in connection with ceremonial requirements, direction, sex, and symbolism of precious stones. Repetition is extensive, most often used in pairs, fourfold with multiples, or fivefold. In weaving words, as well as in tangible representation in painting, the Navajo make full and clever use of contrast.

Although Navajo plastic art, like most art of the American Indians, lacks perspective; unlike much of the art of other tribes, the religious art achieves unity through symbolism. Symbolism, since it is not generally understood, cannot make up for other strictly artistic principles, such as balance, symmetry and contrast. All of these are used in connection with the strain for symbolic representation and the result is satisfactory even to one who does not understand Navajo meanings.

The effect of Navajo art is secured by a use of basic principles, obvious and simple at a casual glance, built up by careful selection of details to which the most thoughtful attention is paid. Imagination knows no bounds in the choosing of such details and it extends to abstract ideas which are made tangible by the most extraordinary symbols. In addition to the enjoyment a spectator may realize from examination of the paintings there is the constant element of surprise at the apparent simplicity, distinction and real sophistication of the thoughtfulness displayed, and particularly at the skill with which the ideas are carried out. In the entire complex the aesthetic is so closely involved with the religious that there is no possibility of separating the two. Rather we should be inclined to conclude that Navajo religion is one of the many examples which illustrate the fact that religion and aesthetics may be one and the same thing.

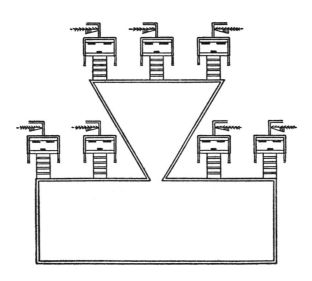

PLATE I

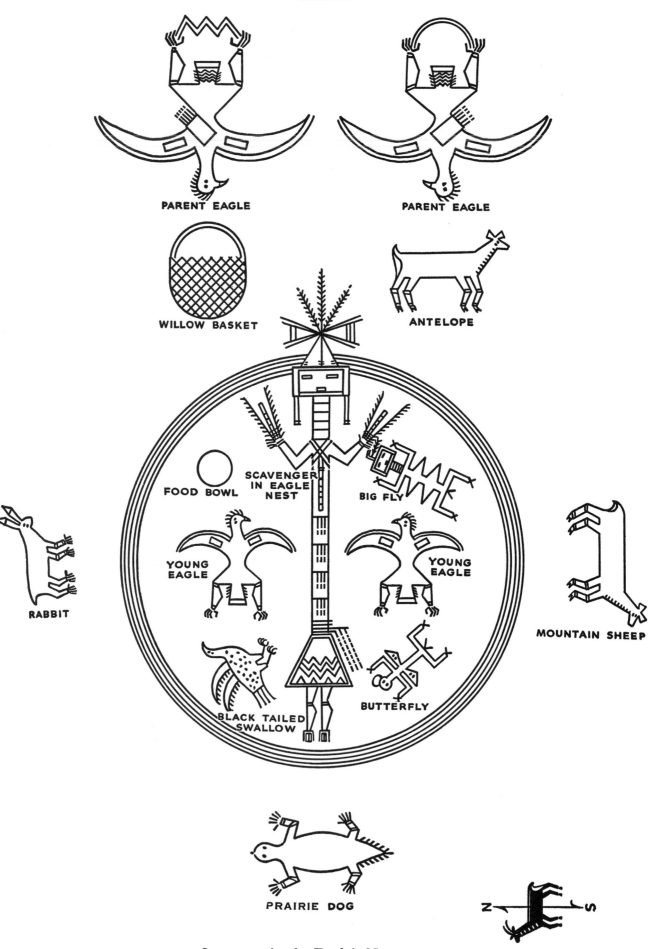

PARENT EAGLE

PARENT EAGLE

WILLOW BASKET

ANTELOPE

FOOD BOWL

SCAVENGER IN EAGLE NEST

BIG FLY

RABBIT

YOUNG EAGLE

YOUNG EAGLE

MOUNTAIN SHEEP

BLACK TAILED SWALLOW

BUTTERFLY

PRAIRIE DOG

Scavenger in the Eagle's Nest

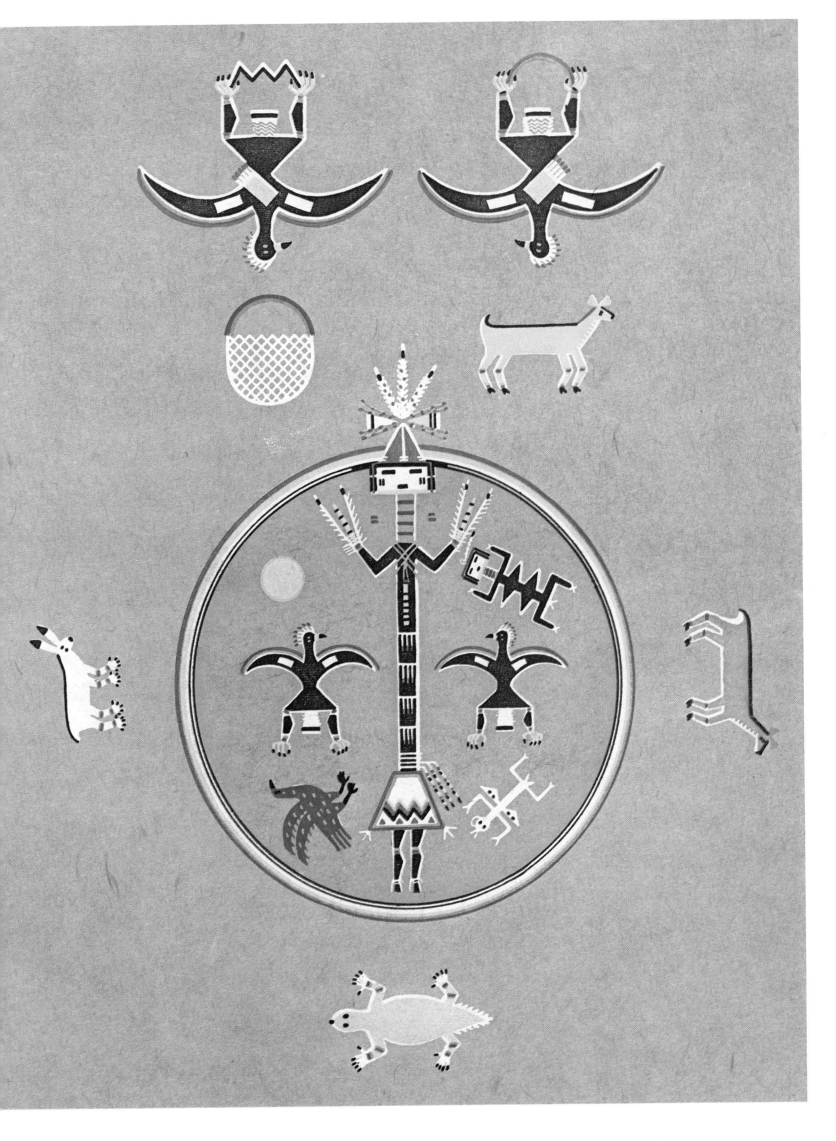

PLATE II

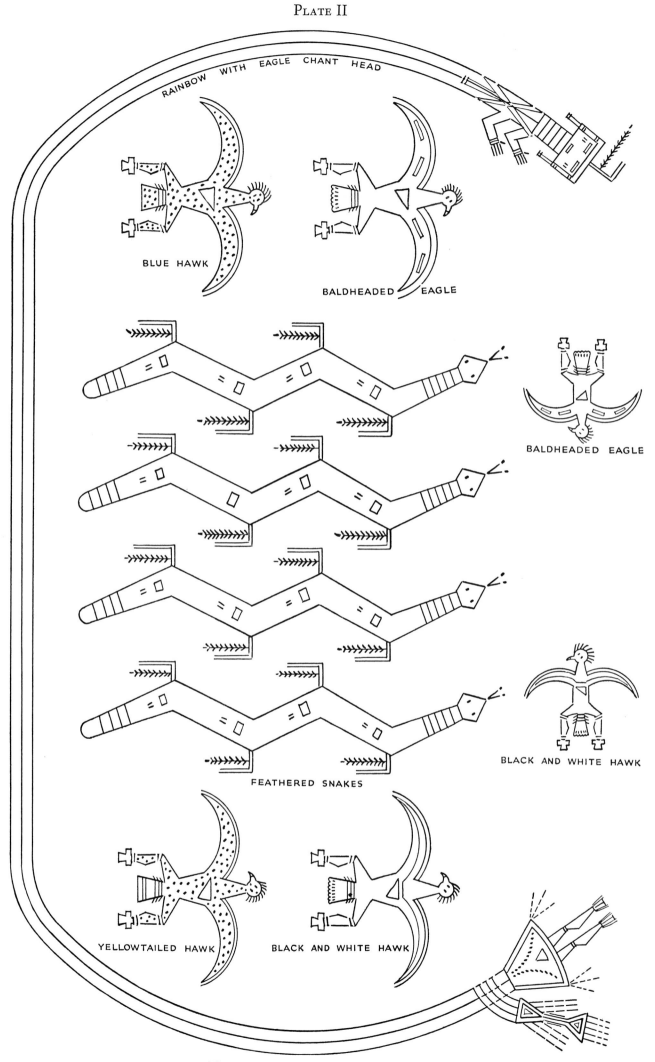

RAINBOW WITH EAGLE CHANT HEAD

BLUE HAWK

BALDHEADED EAGLE

BALDHEADED EAGLE

FEATHERED SNAKES

BLACK AND WHITE HAWK

YELLOWTAILED HAWK

BLACK AND WHITE HAWK

The Snakes Assist in the Ascension

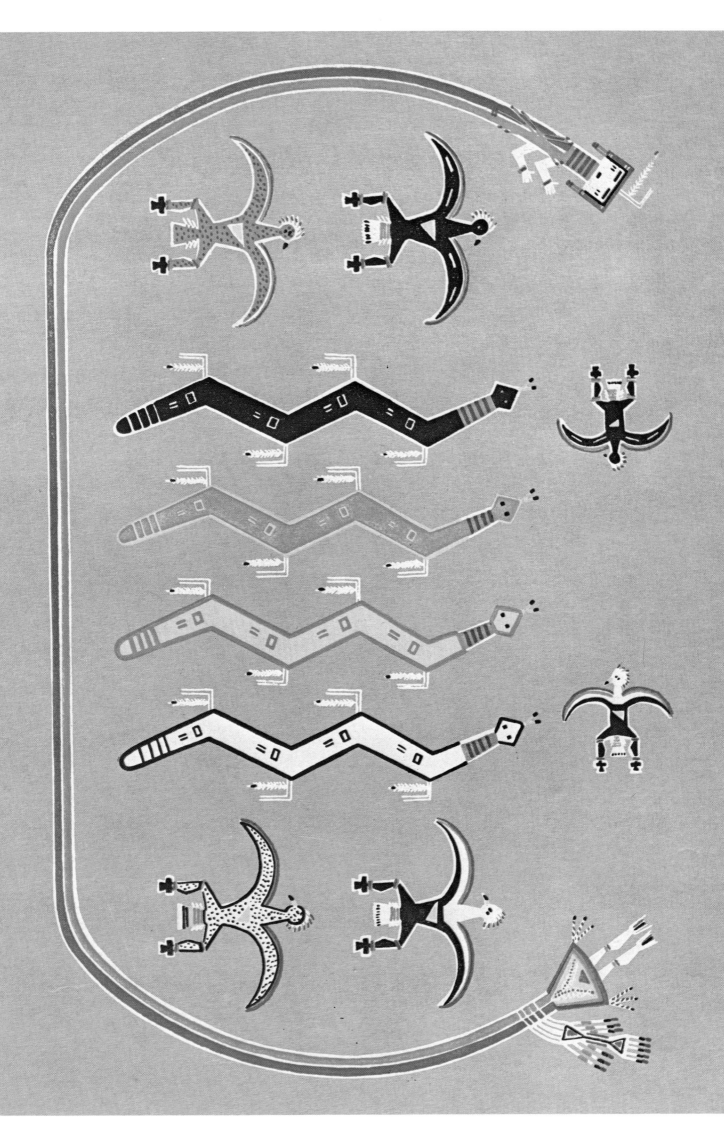

PLATE III

SNAKE WITH BIRD POWER

BLACK AND WHITE
EAGLES

BIG BLACK
HAWKS

WHITE HAWKS

BIG BLUE
HAWKS

YELLOWTAILED
HAWKS

BALDHEADED
EAGLES

RAINBOW ROPE

LIGHTNING ROPE

RAINBOW ROPE

SCAVENGER   ASSISTED   BY   SNAKES

SNAKES   WITH   BIRD   POWER

ZIG-ZAG LIGHTNING ROPE

LIGHTNING ROPE

RAINBOW ROPE

BLACK AND WHITE
EAGLES

BIG BLACK
HAWKS

WHITE HAWKS

BIG BLUE
HAWKS

YELLOWTAILED
HAWKS

BALDHEADED
EAGLES

SNAKE WITH BIRD POWER

The Snakes Lift Scavenger through the Skyhole

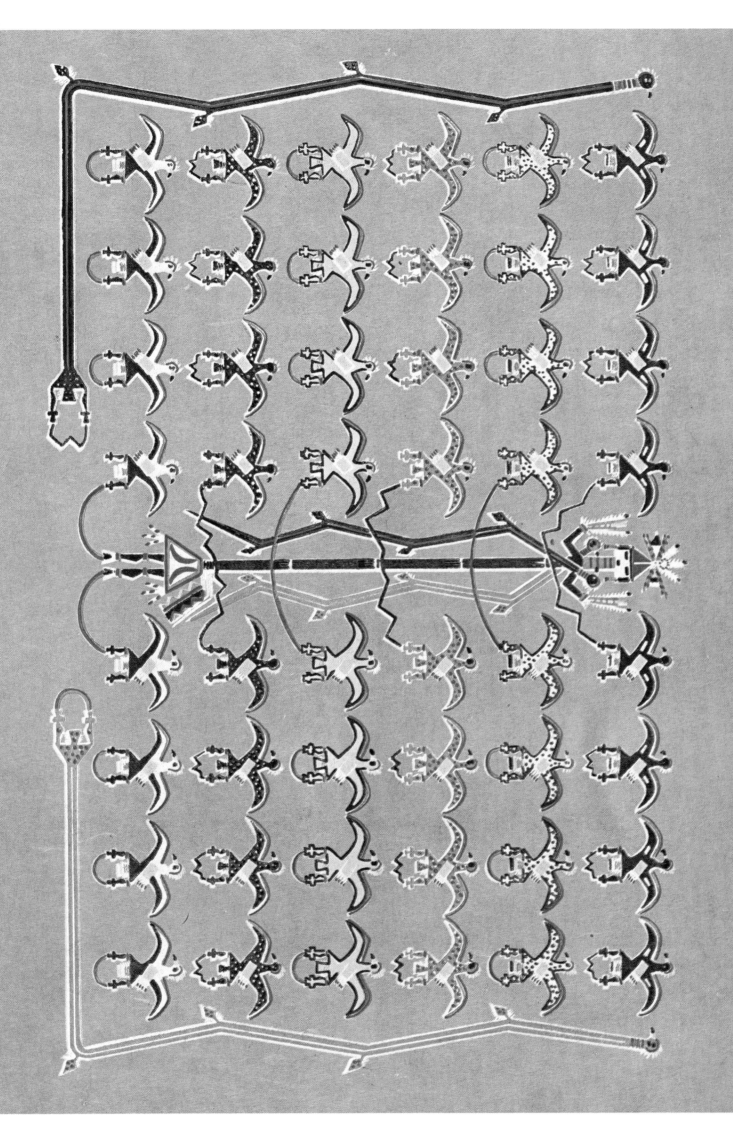

PLATE IV

RAIN STREAMER

BIG BLACK HAWK   WHITE HAWK   BIG BLUE HAWK   YELLOW TAILED HAWK

YELLOW CORN   WHITE CORN

BLACK AND WHITE EAGLE

BLUE HAWKS HOUSE

BLACK HOUSE OF BLACK HAWKS AND EAGLES

BALDHEADED EAGLE

HOUSE OF YELLOW TAILED HAWKS

WHITE HOUSE OF BALDHEADED EAGLES

BLACK AND WHITE EAGLE

YELLOW CORN   WHITE CORN

BALDHEADED EAGLE

BIG BLACK HAWK   WHITE HAWK   BIG BLUE HAWK   YELLOW TAILED HAWK

The Home of the Eagles

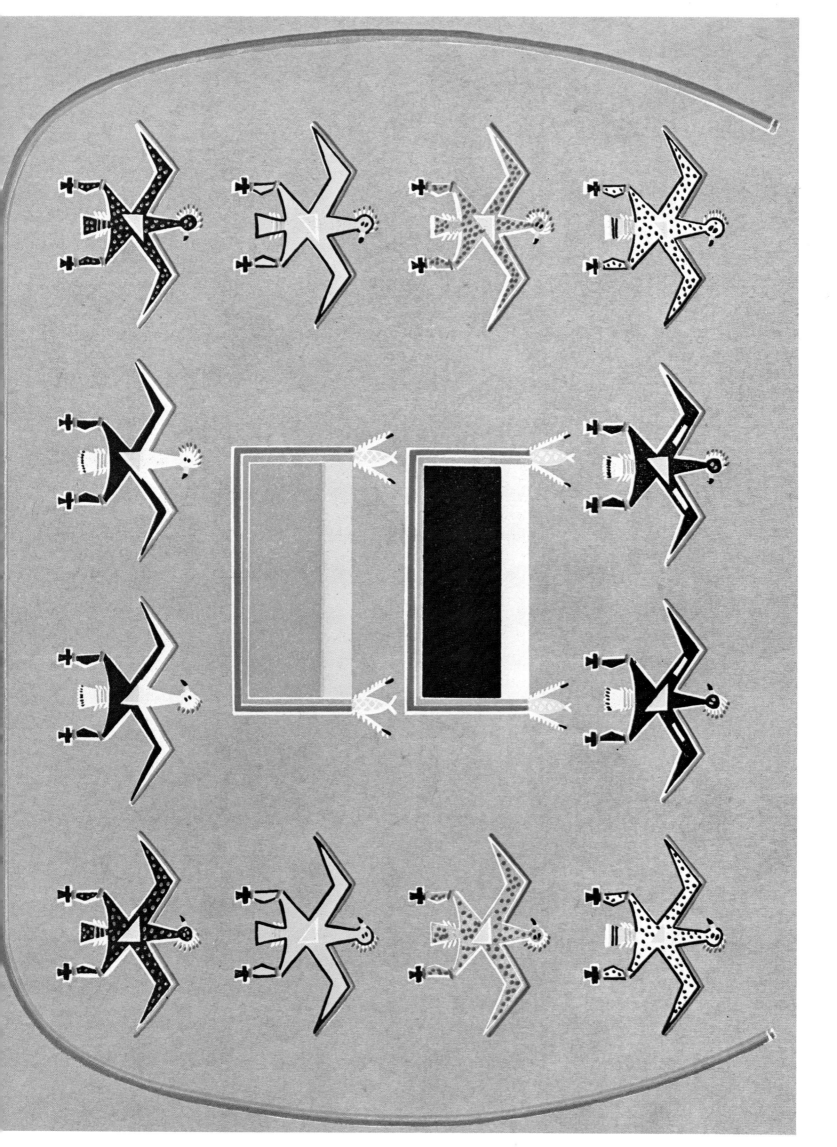

PLATE V

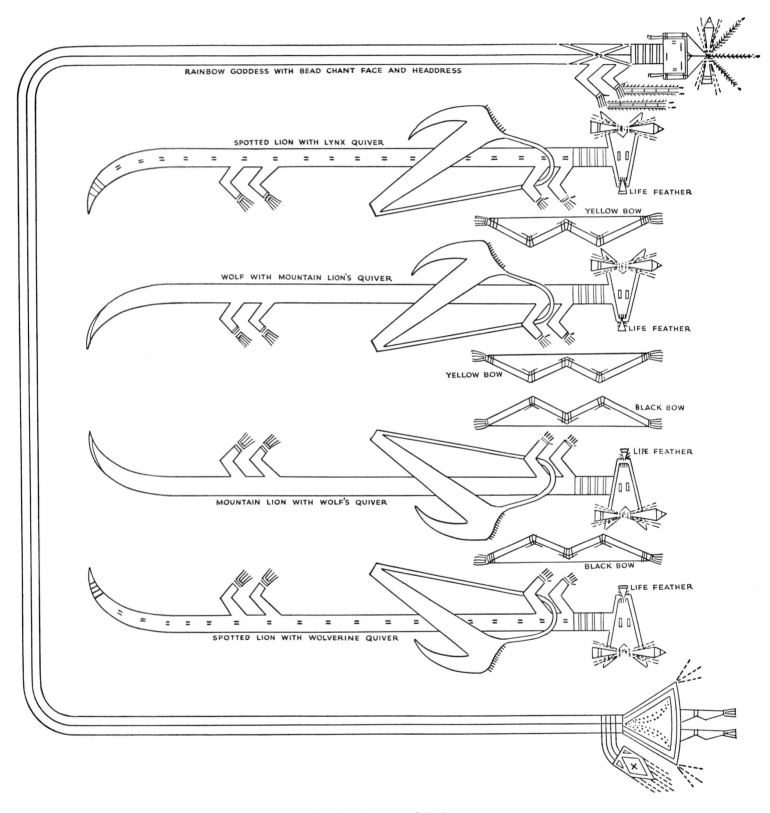

RAINBOW GODDESS WITH BEAD CHANT FACE AND HEADDRESS

SPOTTED LION WITH LYNX QUIVER

LIFE FEATHER

YELLOW BOW

WOLF WITH MOUNTAIN LION'S QUIVER

LIFE FEATHER

YELLOW BOW

BLACK BOW

LIFE FEATHER

MOUNTAIN LION WITH WOLF'S QUIVER

BLACK BOW

LIFE FEATHER

SPOTTED LION WITH WOLVERINE QUIVER

The Exchange of Quivers

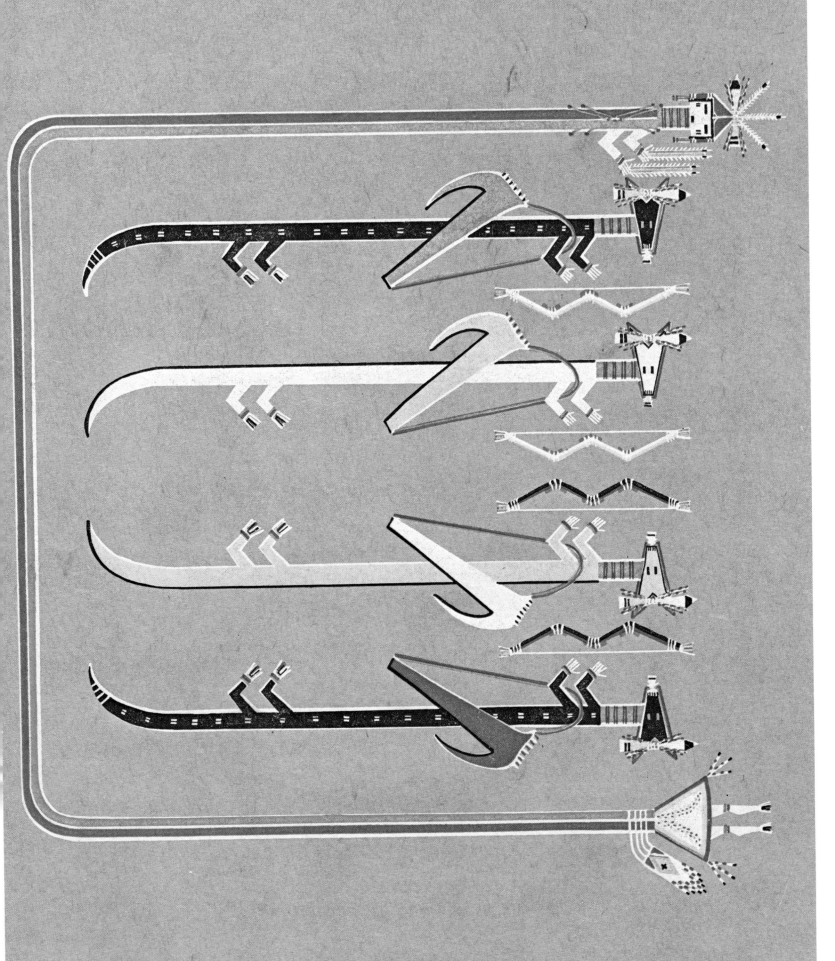

PLATE VI

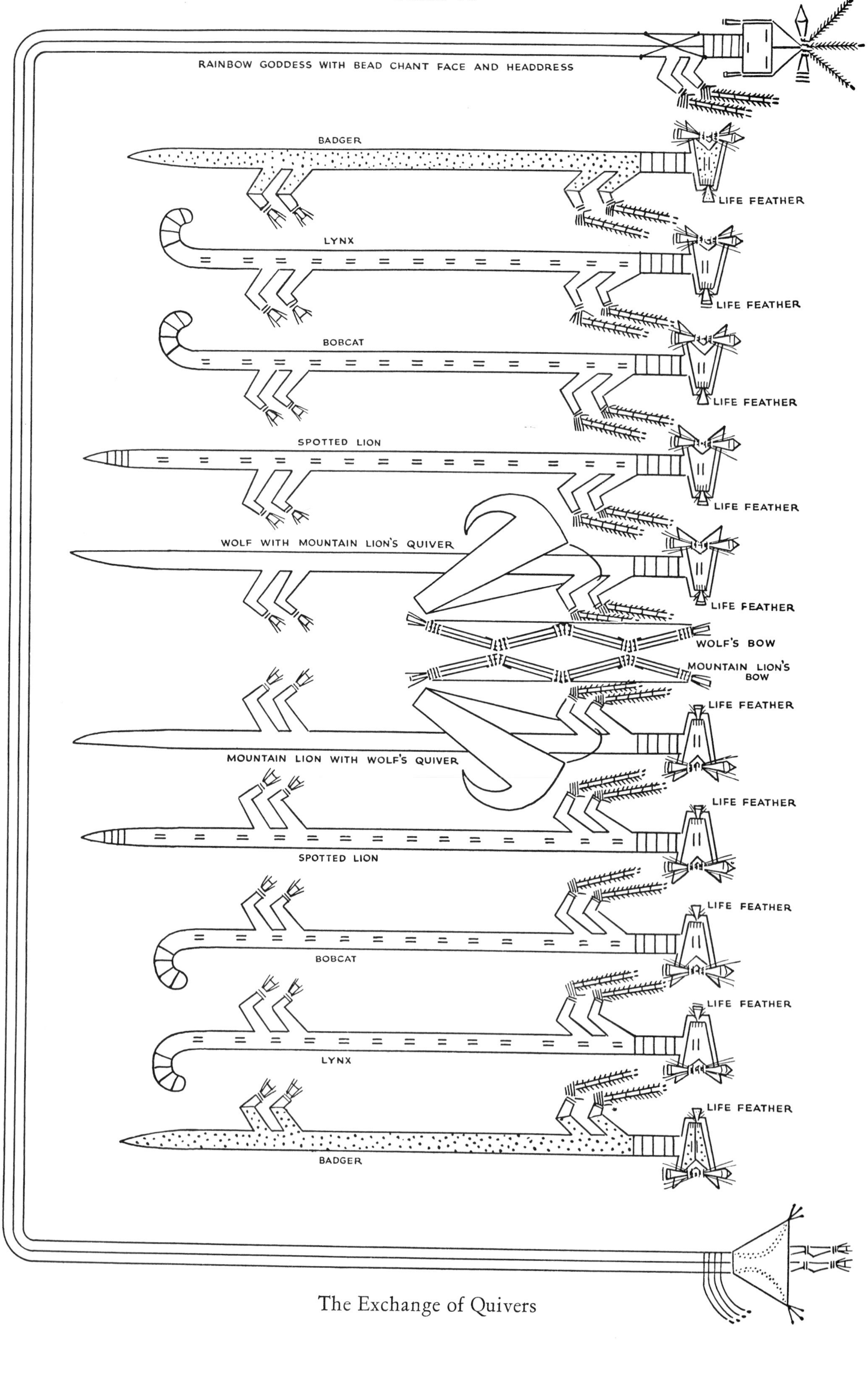

RAINBOW GODDESS WITH BEAD CHANT FACE AND HEADDRESS

BADGER

LIFE FEATHER

LYNX

LIFE FEATHER

BOBCAT

LIFE FEATHER

SPOTTED LION

LIFE FEATHER

WOLF WITH MOUNTAIN LION'S QUIVER

LIFE FEATHER

WOLF'S BOW

MOUNTAIN LION'S BOW

LIFE FEATHER

MOUNTAIN LION WITH WOLF'S QUIVER

LIFE FEATHER

SPOTTED LION

LIFE FEATHER

BOBCAT

LIFE FEATHER

LYNX

LIFE FEATHER

BADGER

LIFE FEATHER

The Exchange of Quivers

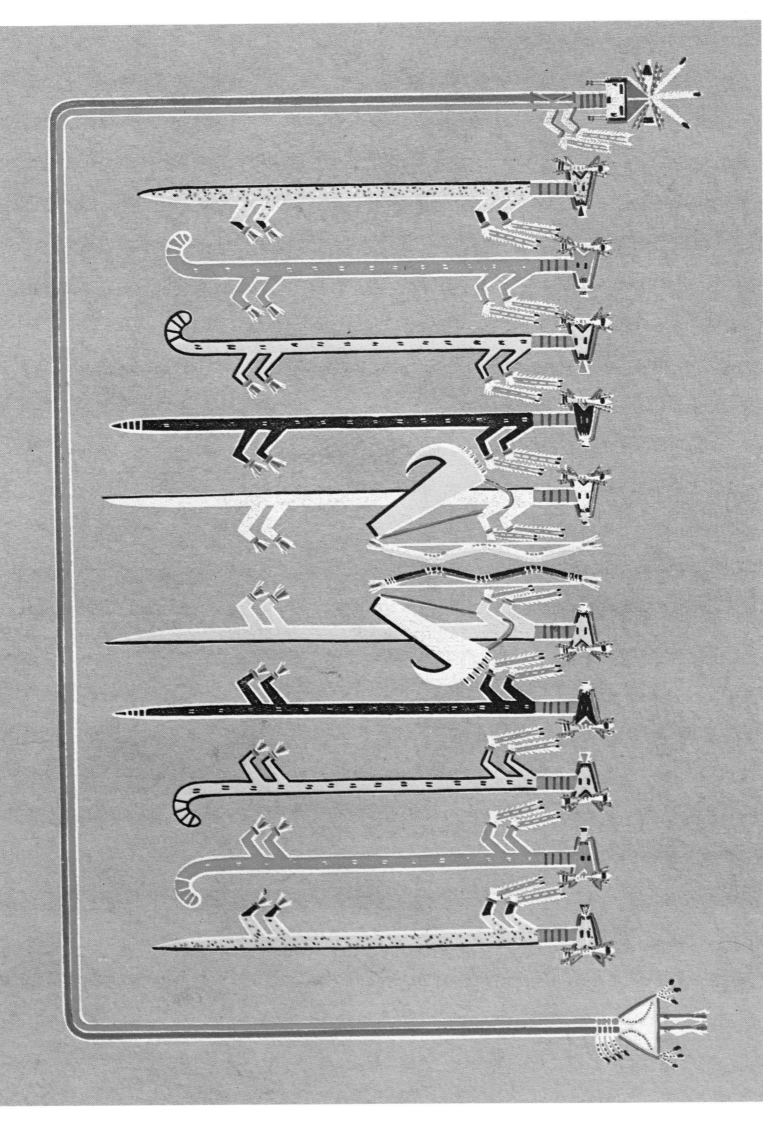

PLATE VII

RAINBOW GODDESS WITH BEAD CHANT FACE AND HEADDRESS

BADGER WITH CORN PACKS

LYNX WITH CORN PACKS

BOBCAT WITH CORN PACKS

SPOTTED LION WITH CORN PACKS

WOLF WITH CORN PACKS

MOUNTAIN LION WITH CORN PACKS

SPOTTED LION WITH CORN PACKS

BOBCAT WITH CORN PACKS

LYNX WITH CORN PACKS

BADGER WITH CORN PACKS

The Hunting Animals with Cornpacks

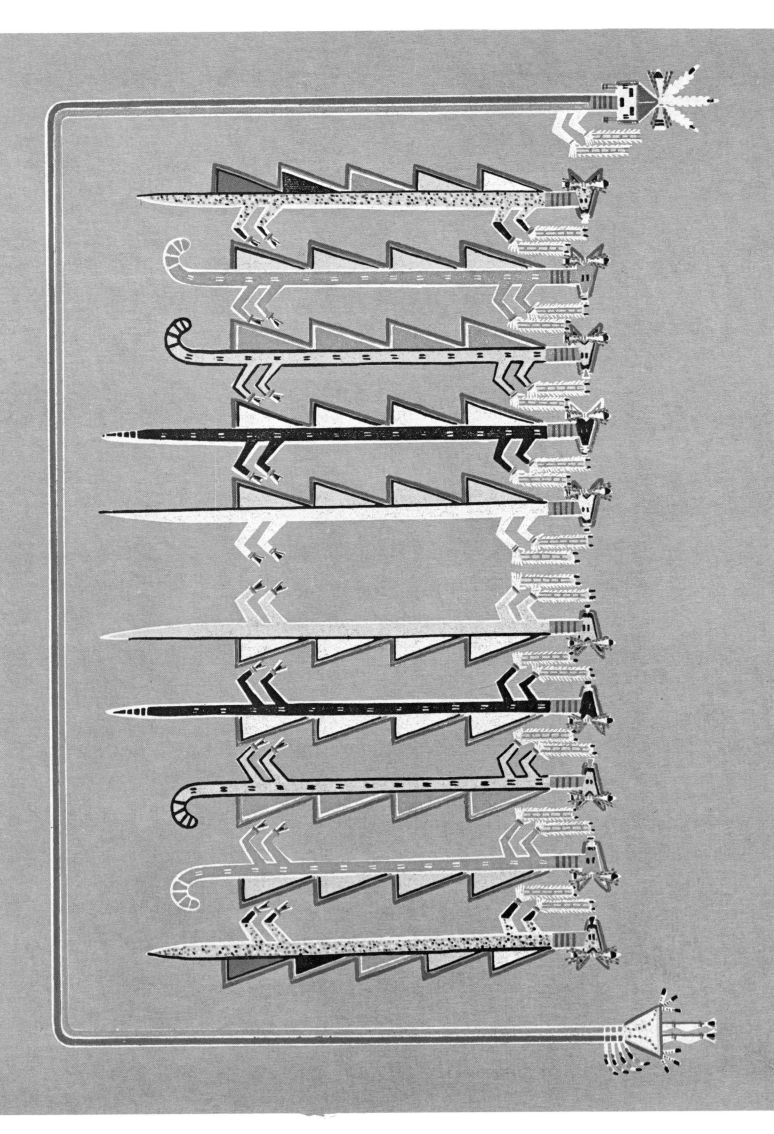

PLATE VIII

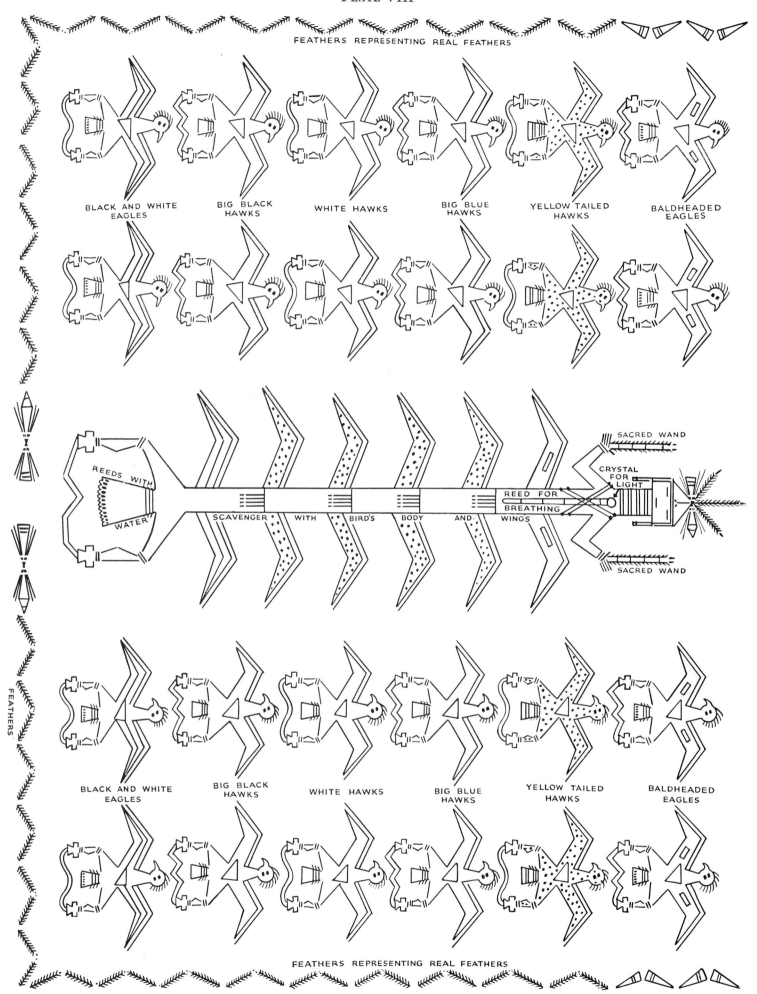

FEATHERS REPRESENTING REAL FEATHERS

BLACK AND WHITE EAGLES

BIG BLACK HAWKS

WHITE HAWKS

BIG BLUE HAWKS

YELLOW TAILED HAWKS

BALDHEADED EAGLES

SACRED WAND

CRYSTAL FOR LIGHT

REEDS WITH WATER

SCAVENGER WITH BIRD'S BODY AND WINGS

REED FOR BREATHING

SACRED WAND

FEATHERS

BLACK AND WHITE EAGLES

BIG BLACK HAWKS

WHITE HAWKS

BIG BLUE HAWKS

YELLOW TAILED HAWKS

BALDHEADED EAGLES

FEATHERS REPRESENTING REAL FEATHERS

The Final Ascension of Scavenger Attended by Eagles

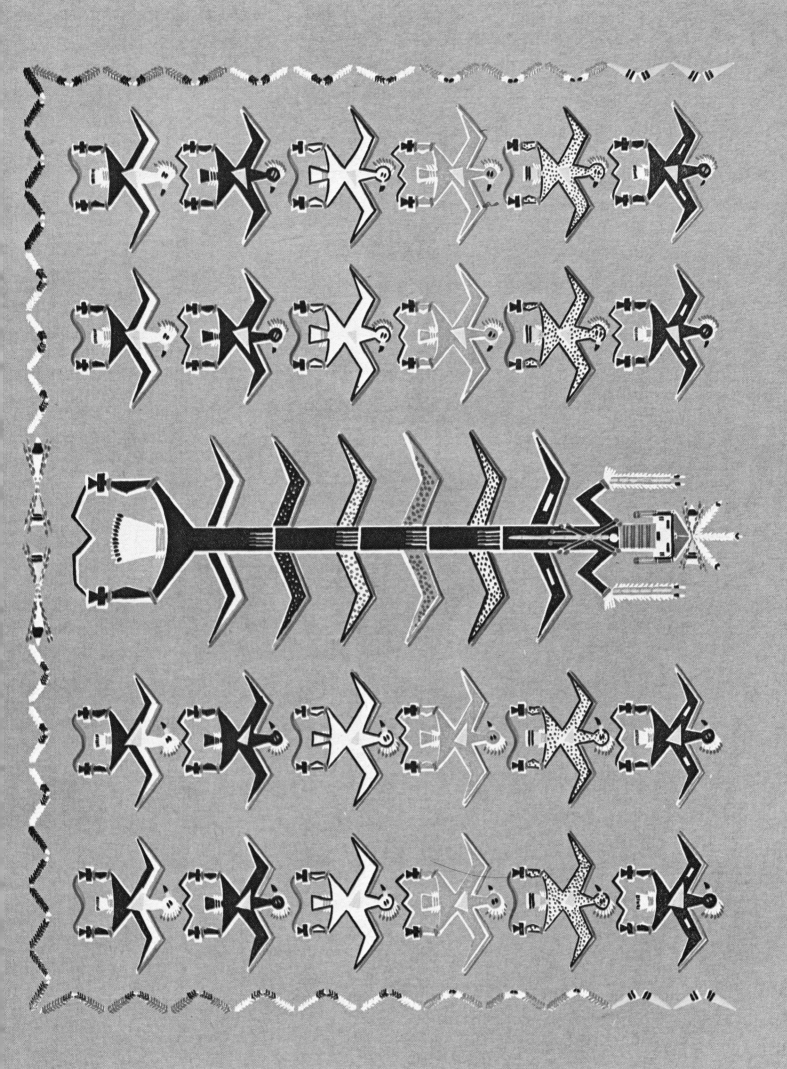

PLATE IX

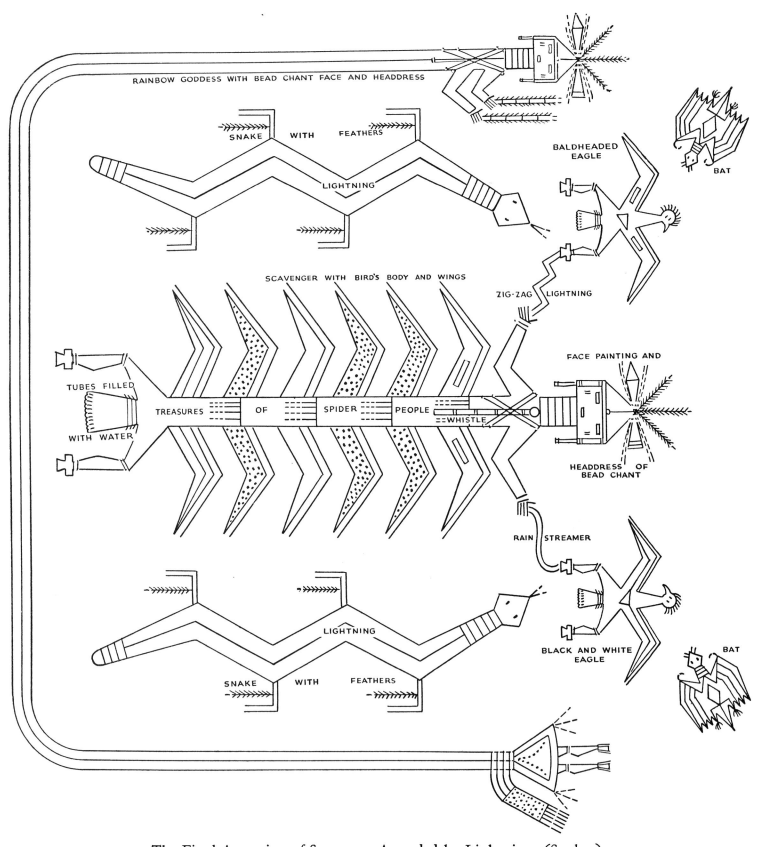

RAINBOW GODDESS WITH BEAD CHANT FACE AND HEADDRESS

SNAKE WITH FEATHERS

LIGHTNING

BALDHEADED EAGLE

BAT

SCAVENGER WITH BIRD'S BODY AND WINGS

ZIG-ZAG LIGHTNING

TUBES FILLED WITH WATER

TREASURES OF SPIDER PEOPLE WHISTLE

FACE PAINTING AND

HEADDRESS OF BEAD CHANT

RAIN STREAMER

LIGHTNING

SNAKE WITH FEATHERS

BLACK AND WHITE EAGLE

BAT

The Final Ascension of Scavenger Attended by Lightnings (Snakes)

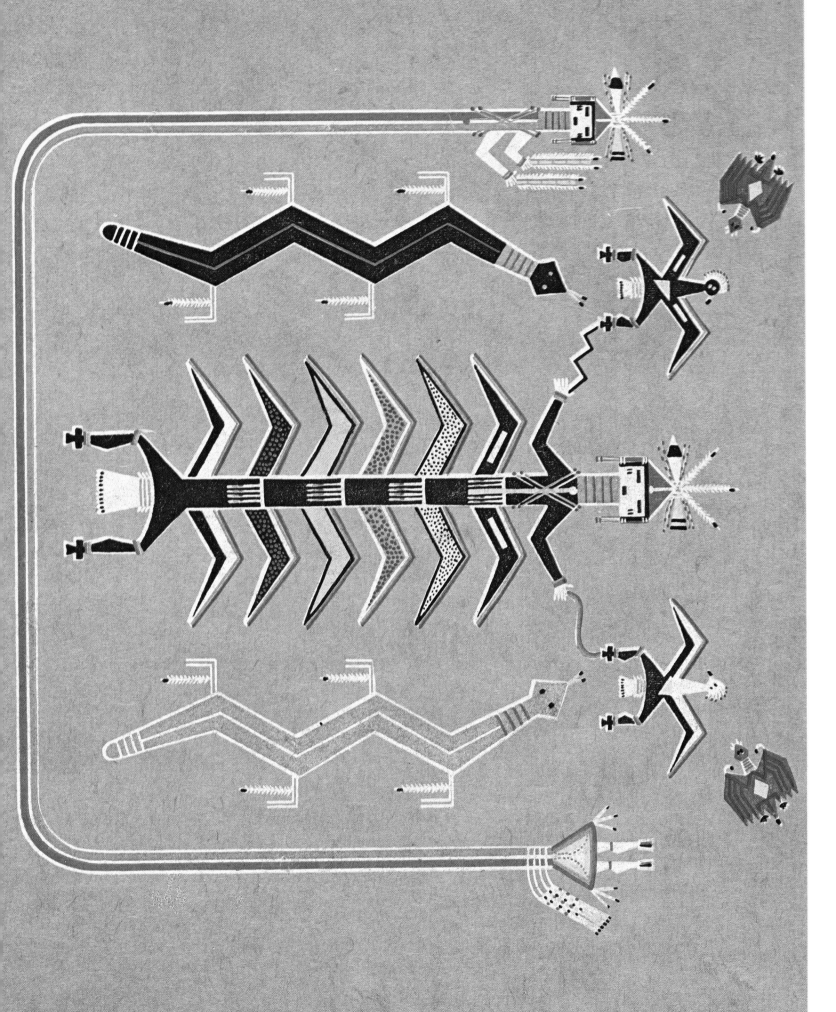

PLATE X

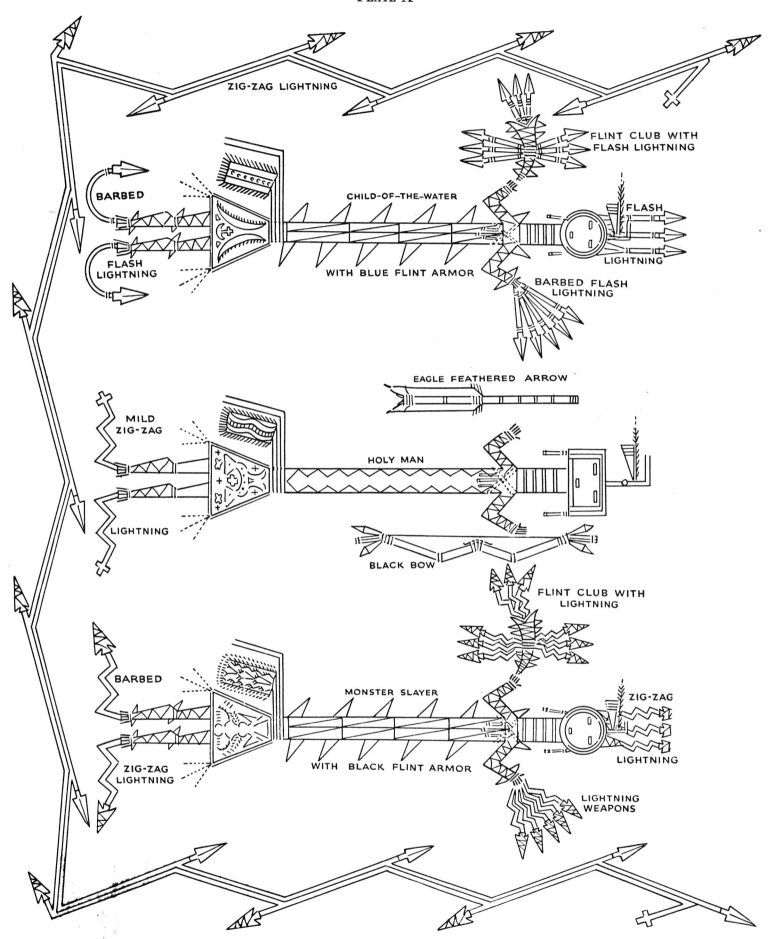

ZIG-ZAG LIGHTNING

FLINT CLUB WITH
FLASH LIGHTNING

BARBED

FLASH
LIGHTNING

CHILD-OF-THE-WATER

WITH BLUE FLINT ARMOR

FLASH

LIGHTNING

BARBED FLASH
LIGHTNING

EAGLE FEATHERED ARROW

MILD
ZIG-ZAG

LIGHTNING

HOLY MAN

BLACK BOW

FLINT CLUB WITH
LIGHTNING

BARBED

ZIG-ZAG
LIGHTNING

MONSTER SLAYER

WITH BLACK FLINT ARMOR

ZIG-ZAG

LIGHTNING

LIGHTNING
WEAPONS

Holy Man Guarded by Monster Slayer and Child-of-the-water

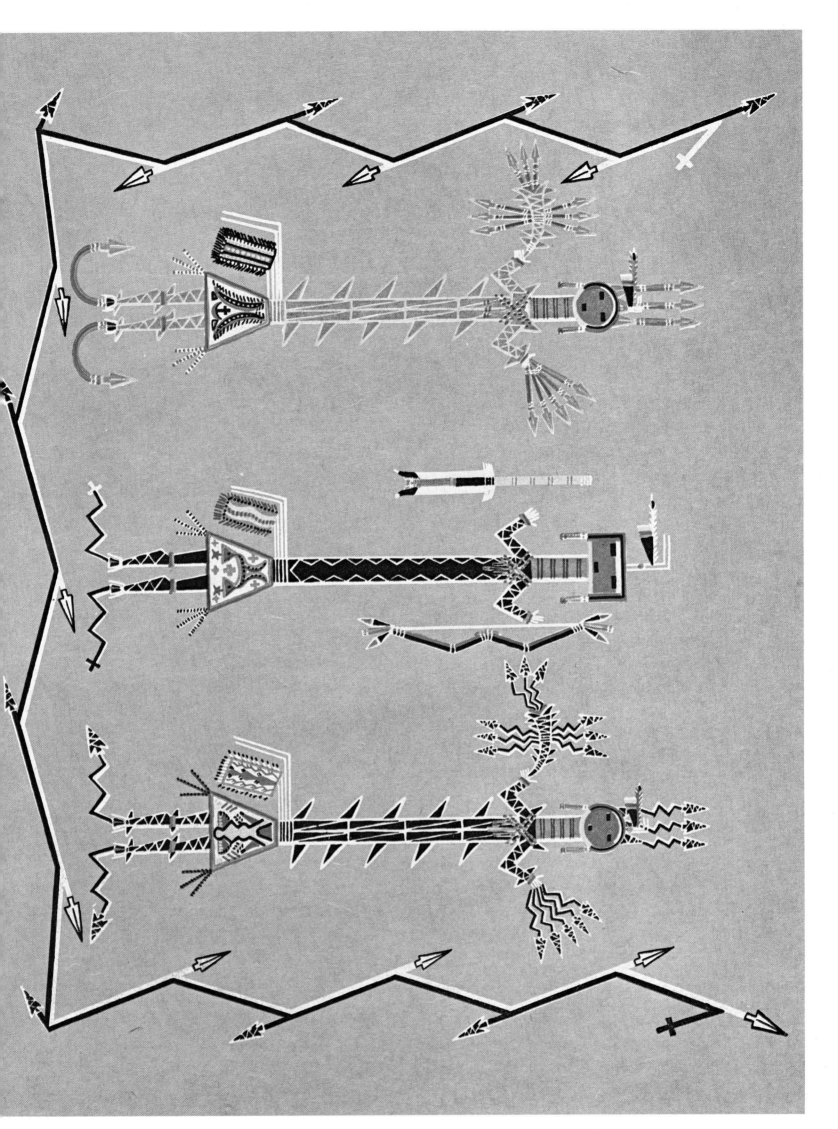

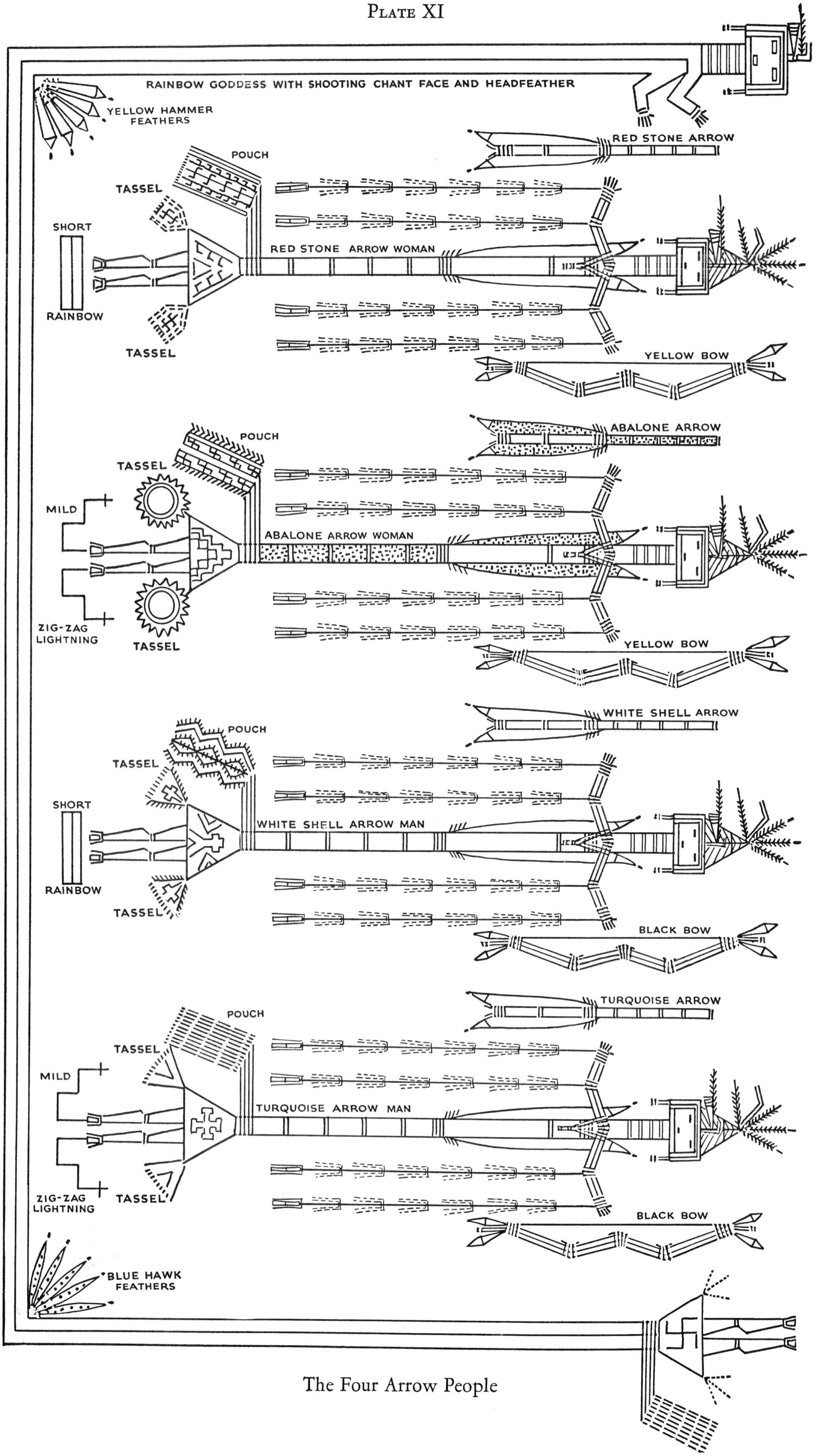

PLATE XI

RAINBOW GODDESS WITH SHOOTING CHANT FACE AND HEADFEATHER

YELLOW HAMMER FEATHERS

RED STONE ARROW

POUCH

TASSEL

SHORT

RED STONE ARROW WOMAN

RAINBOW

TASSEL

YELLOW BOW

POUCH

TASSEL

MILD

ABALONE ARROW

ABALONE ARROW WOMAN

ZIG-ZAG LIGHTNING

TASSEL

YELLOW BOW

POUCH

TASSEL

WHITE SHELL ARROW

SHORT

WHITE SHELL ARROW MAN

RAINBOW

TASSEL

BLACK BOW

POUCH

TASSEL

MILD

TURQUOISE ARROW

TURQUOISE ARROW MAN

ZIG-ZAG LIGHTNING

TASSEL

BLACK BOW

BLUE HAWK FEATHERS

The Four Arrow People

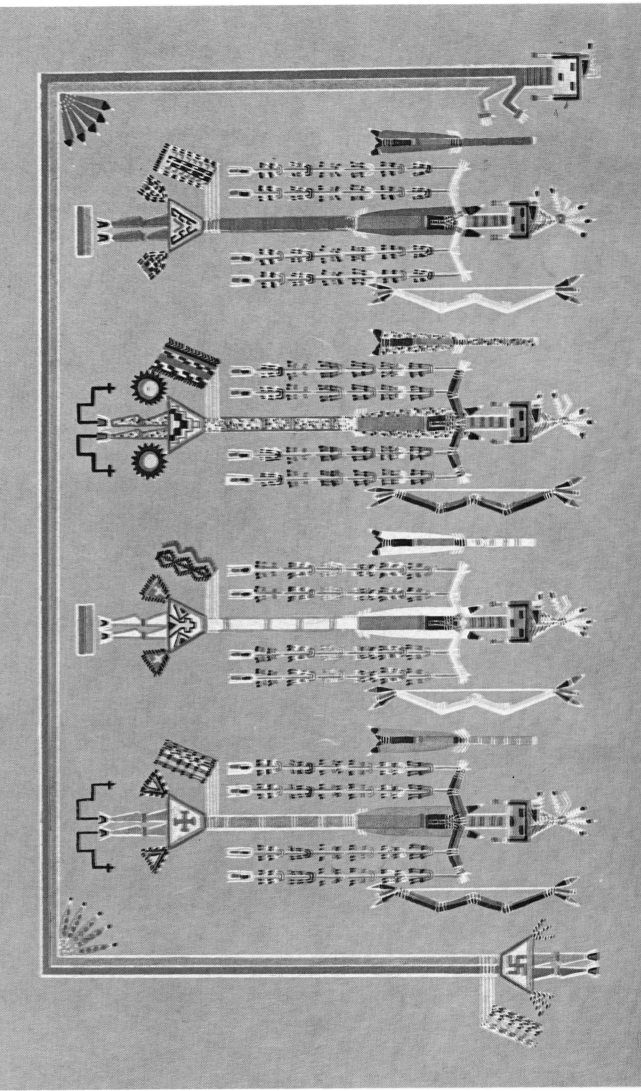

PLATE XII

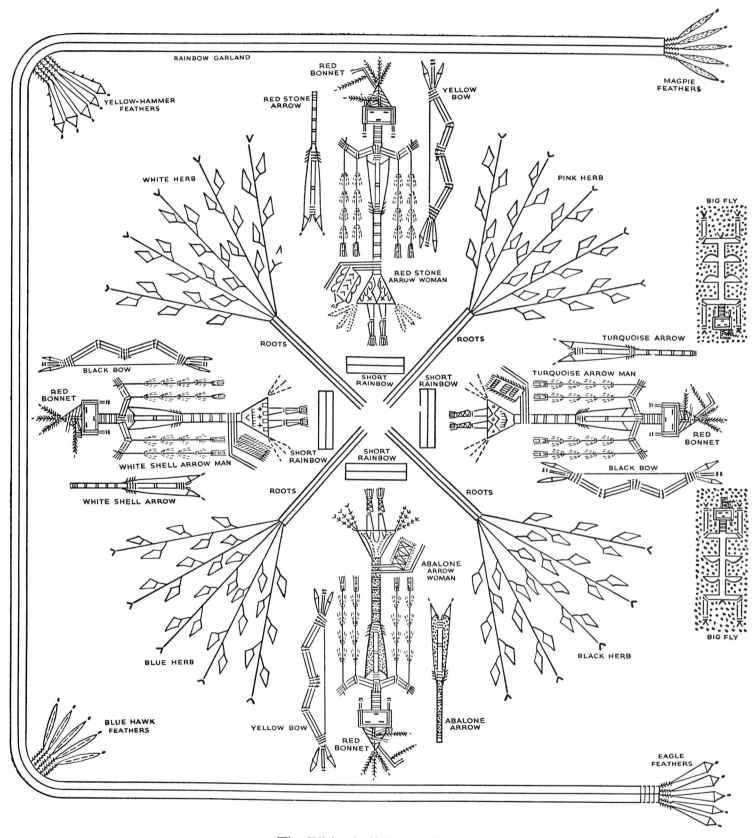

The Whiteshell Arrow People

PLATE XIII

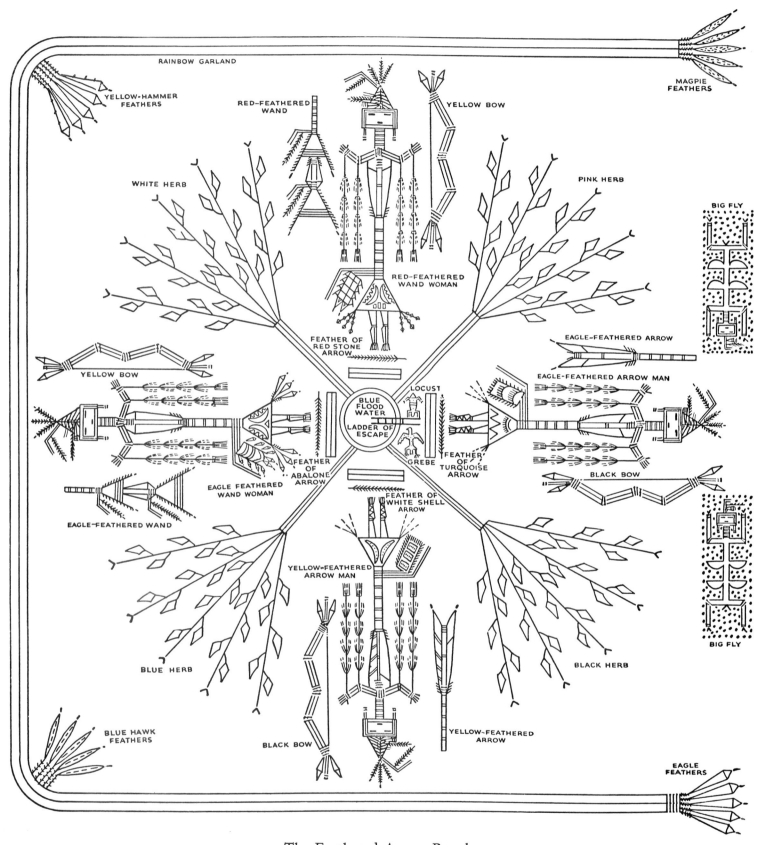

The Feathered Arrow People

PLATE XIV

The Mountain-that-fell-out

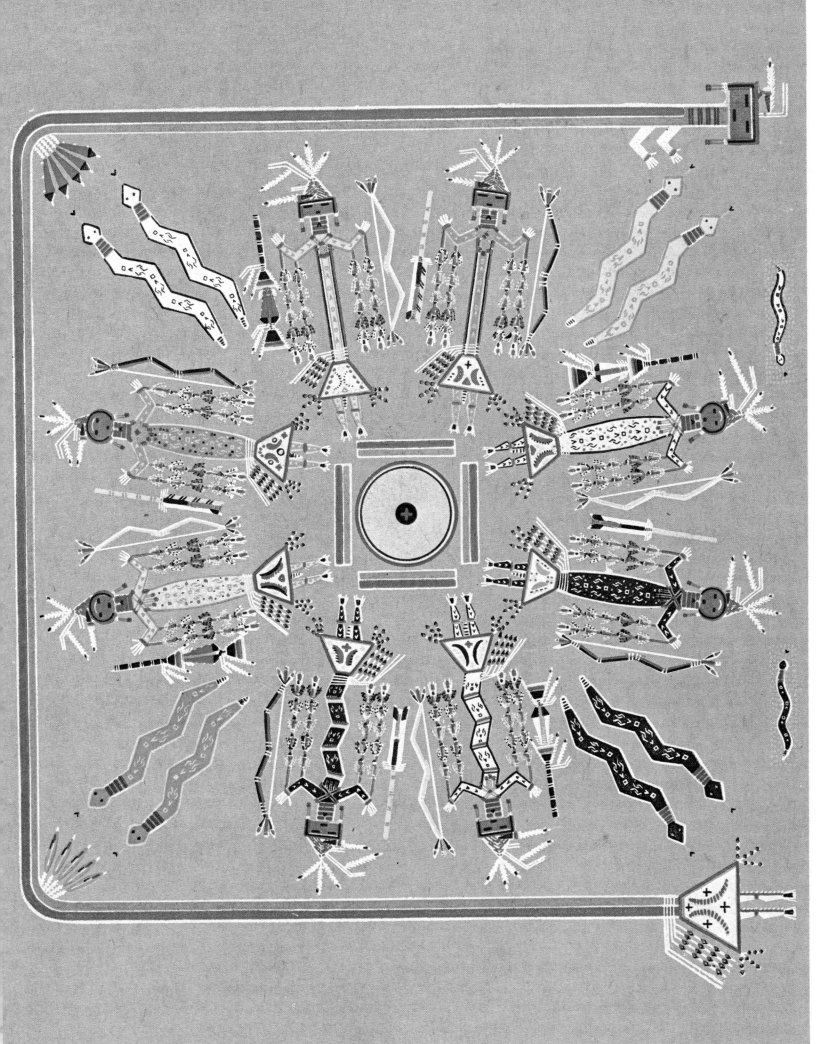

PLATE XV

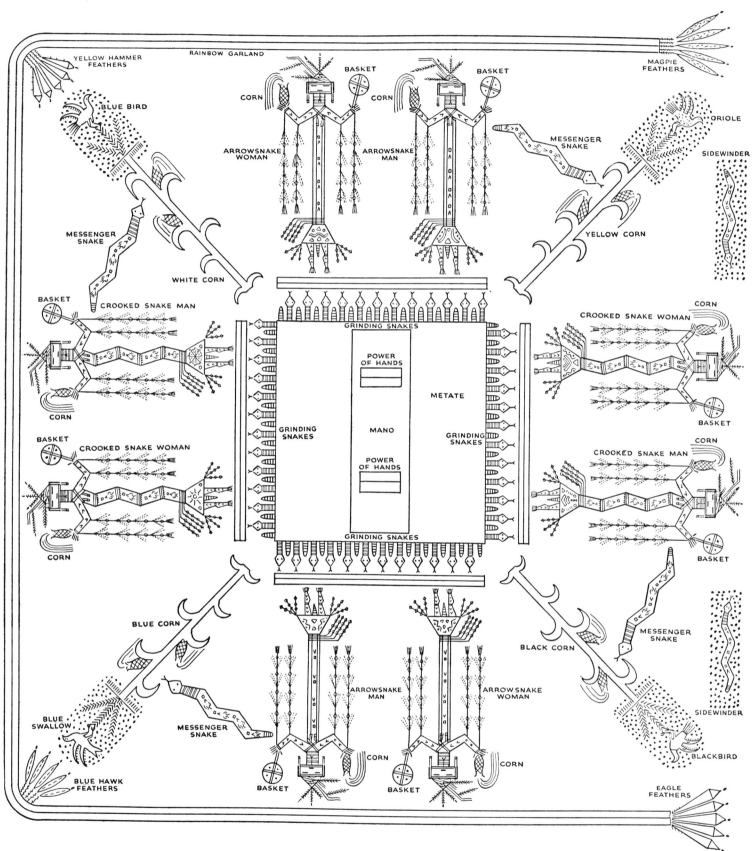

The Grinding Snakes

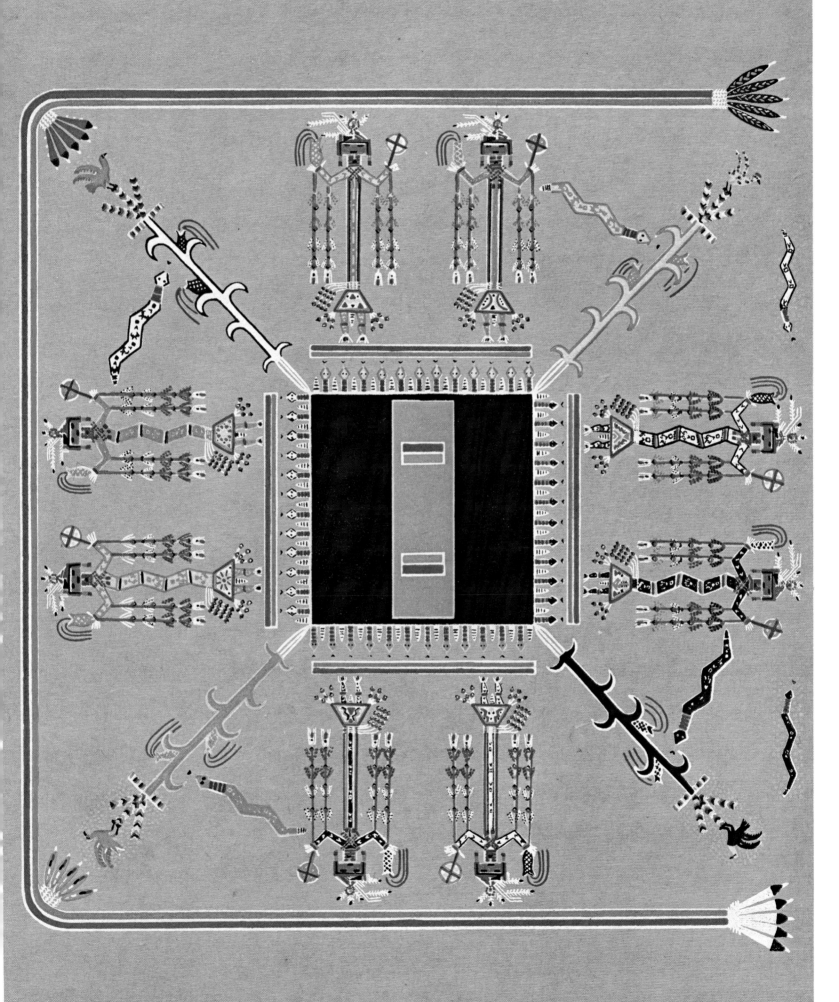

PLATE XVI

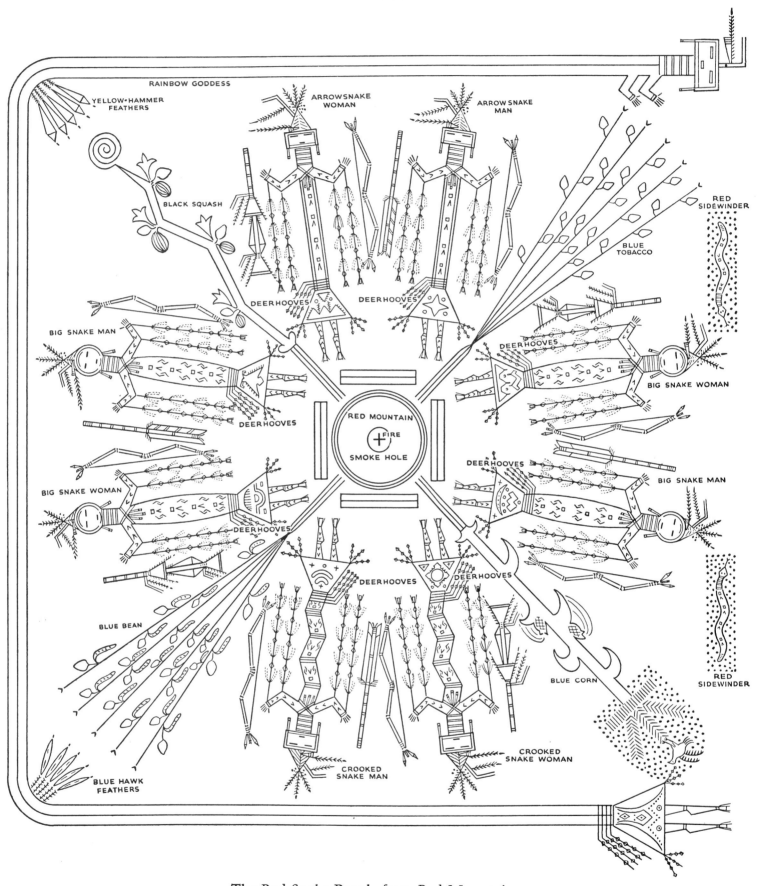

The Red Snake People from Red Mountain

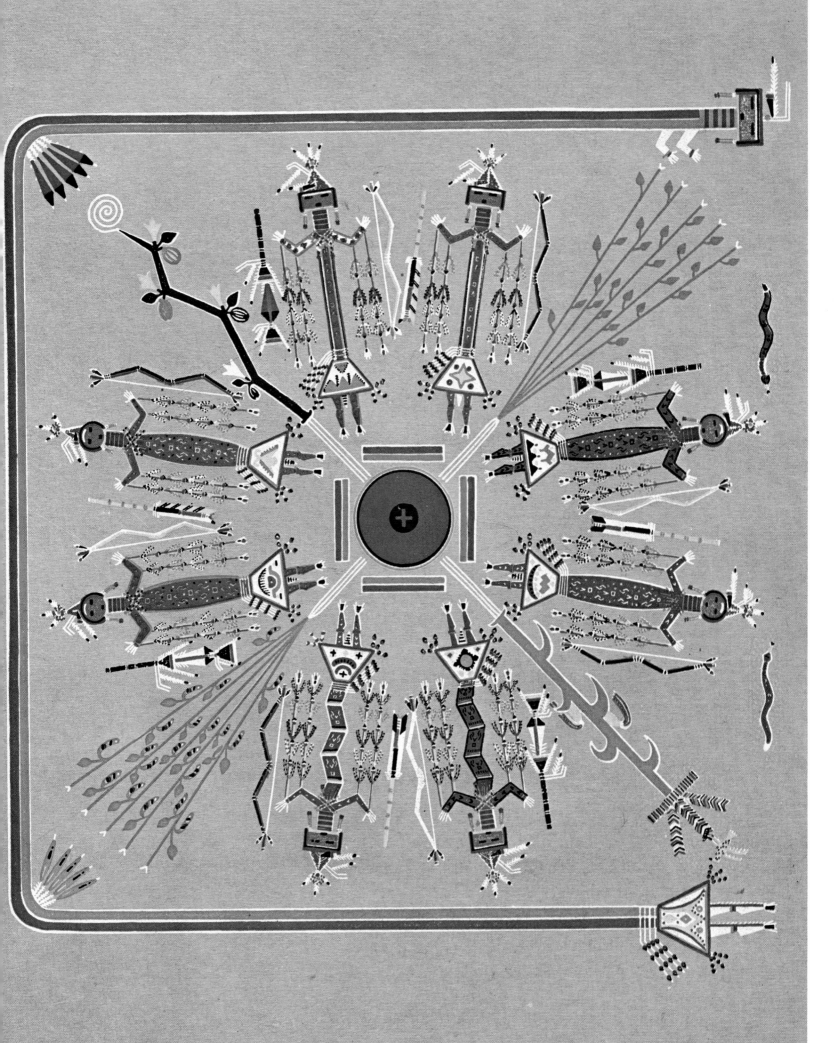

PLATE XVII

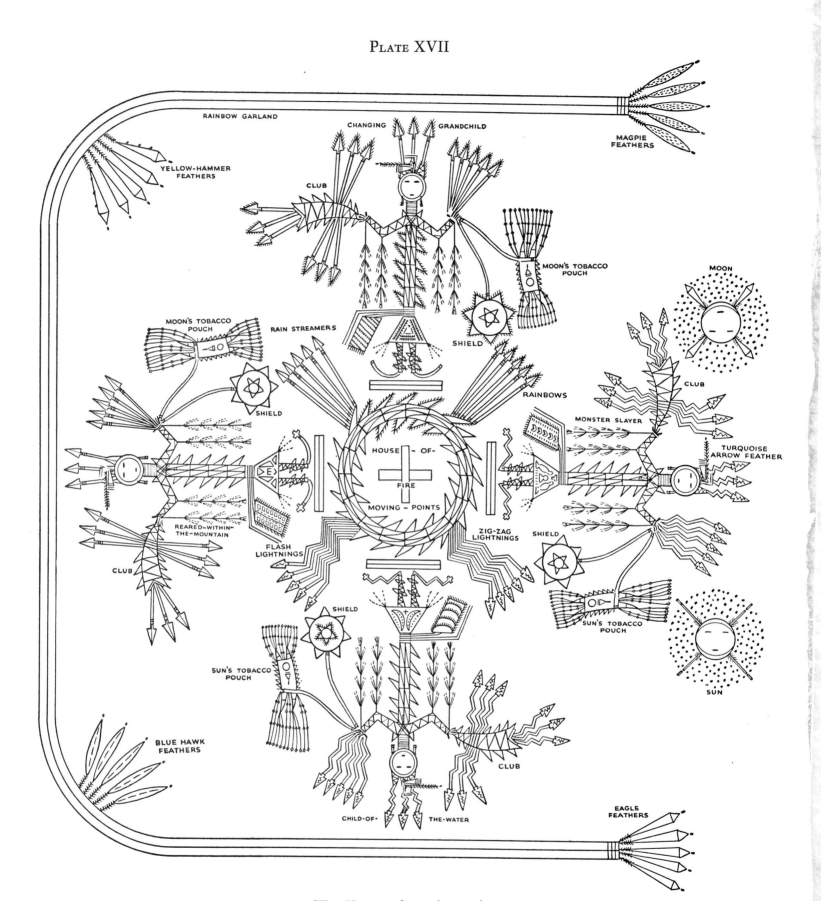

The House-of-moving-points

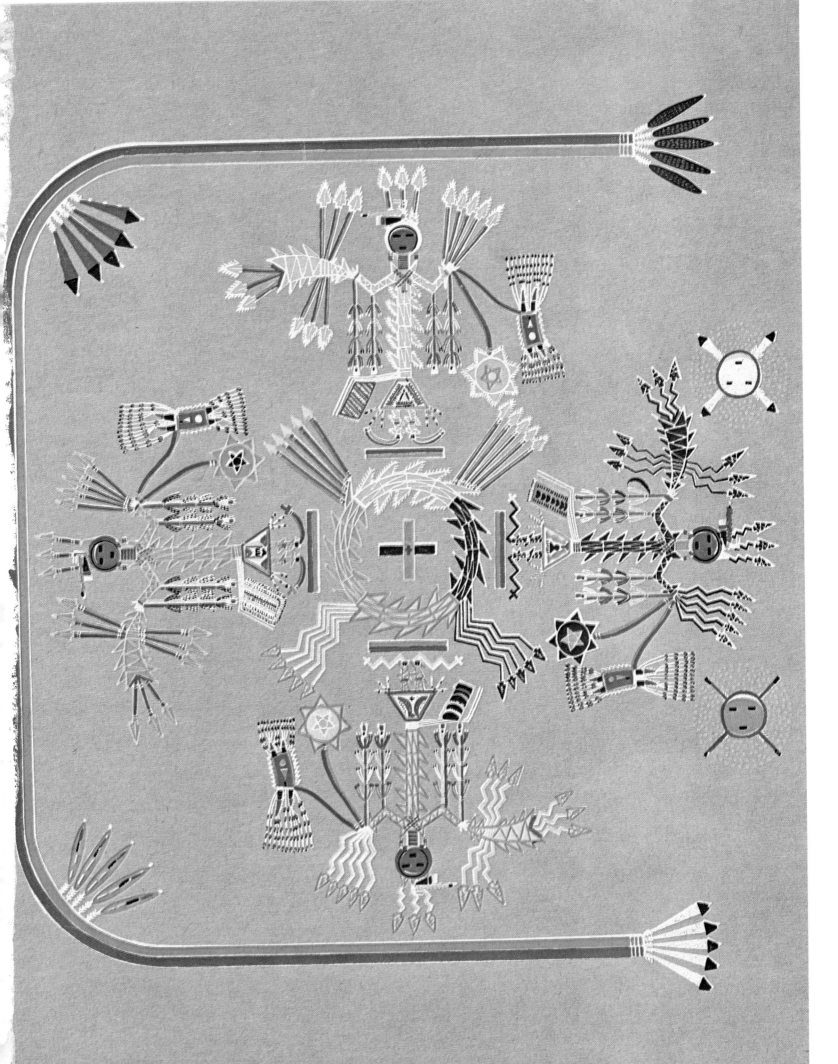

PLATE XVIII

The Four Mountains

PLATE XIX

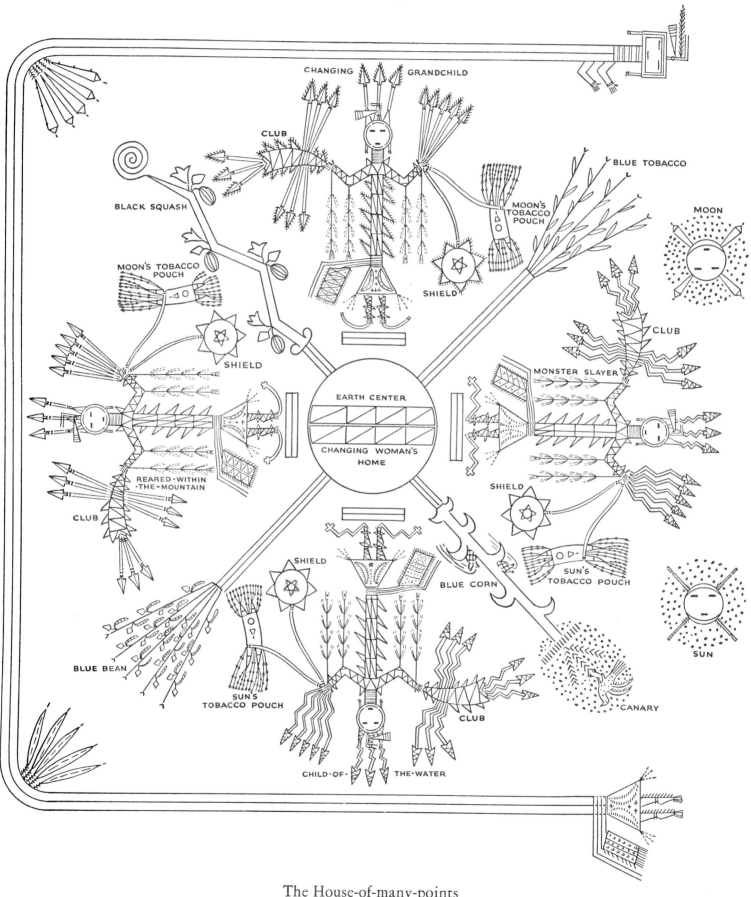

The House-of-many-points

Plate XX

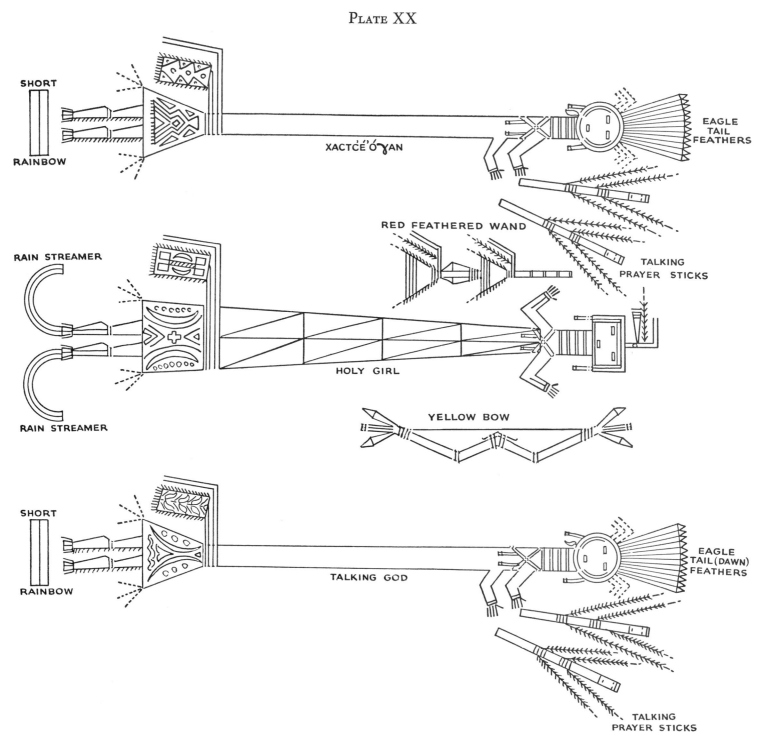

SHORT

RAINBOW

XACTĊÉ'ÓɣAN

EAGLE
TAIL
FEATHERS

RED FEATHERED WAND

TALKING
PRAYER STICKS

RAIN STREAMER

RAIN STREAMER

HOLY GIRL

YELLOW BOW

SHORT

RAINBOW

TALKING GOD

EAGLE
TAIL (DAWN)
FEATHERS

TALKING
PRAYER STICKS

Holy Girl Protected by Talking God and *xactċé'óɣan*

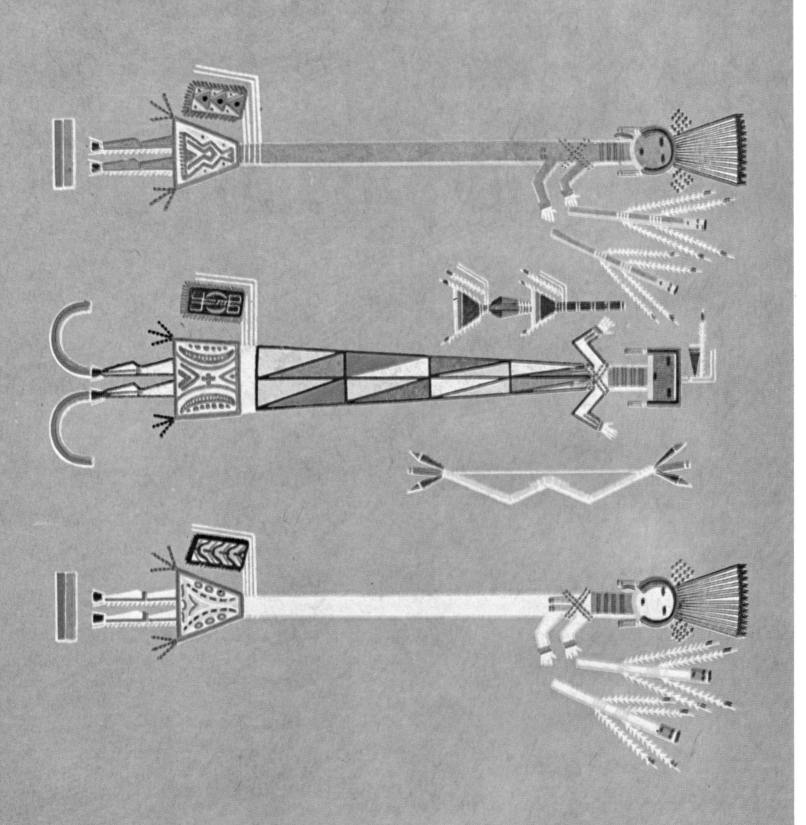

PLATE XXI

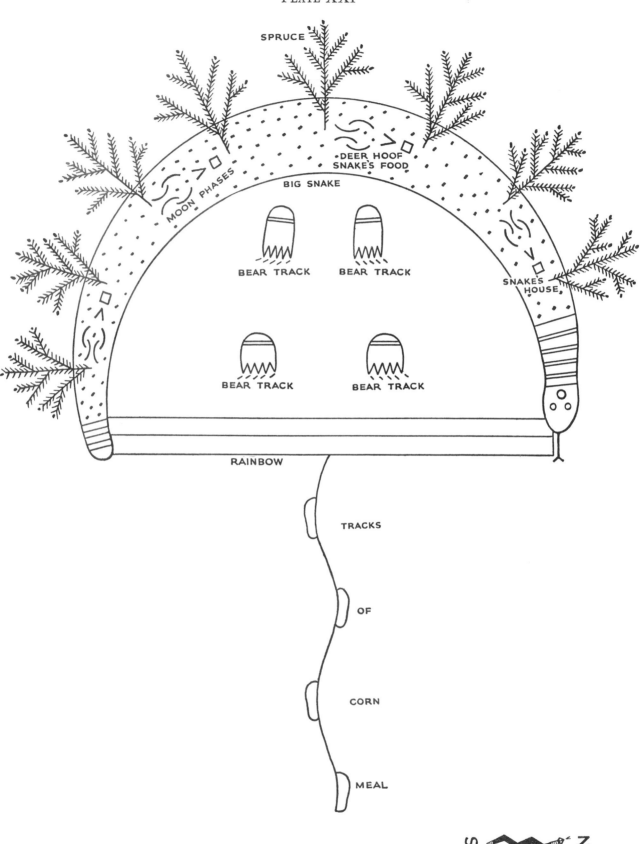

The Shock Painting

PLATE XXII

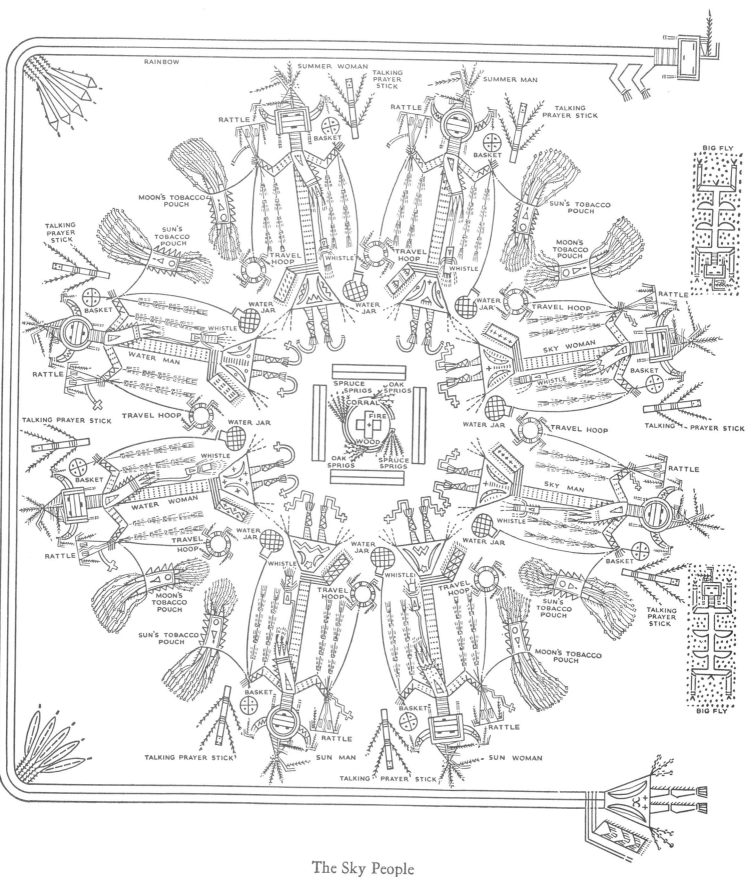

The Sky People

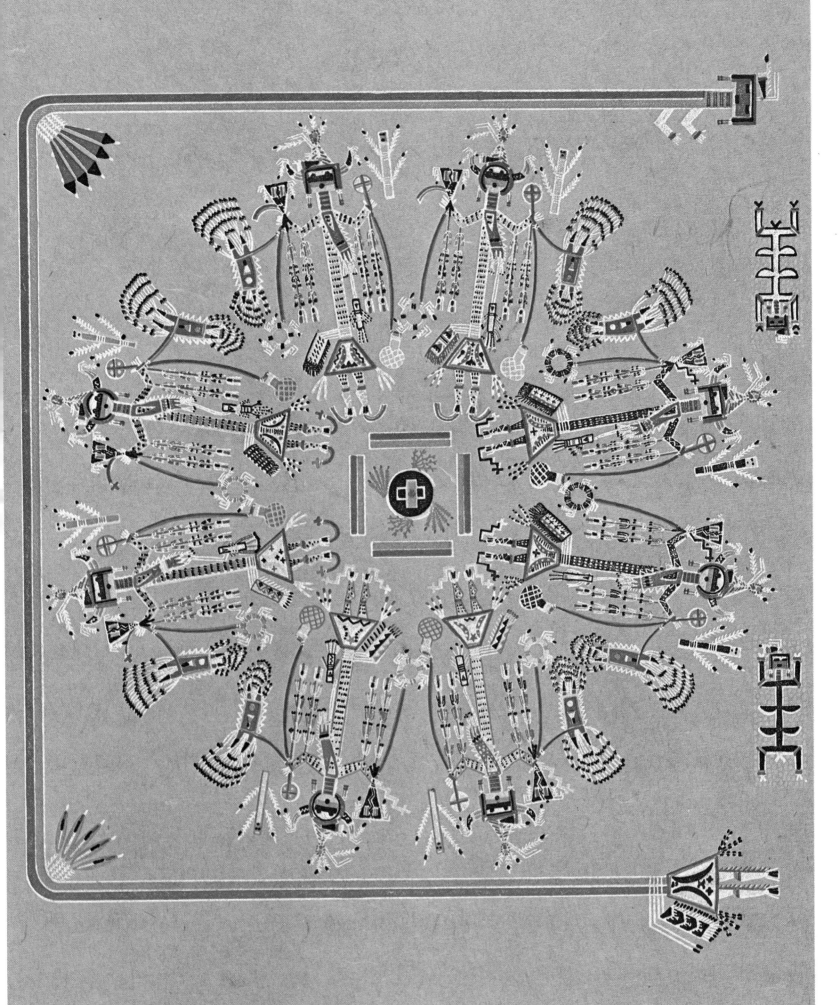

PLATE XXIII

The Home of the Buffalo People

PLATE XXIV

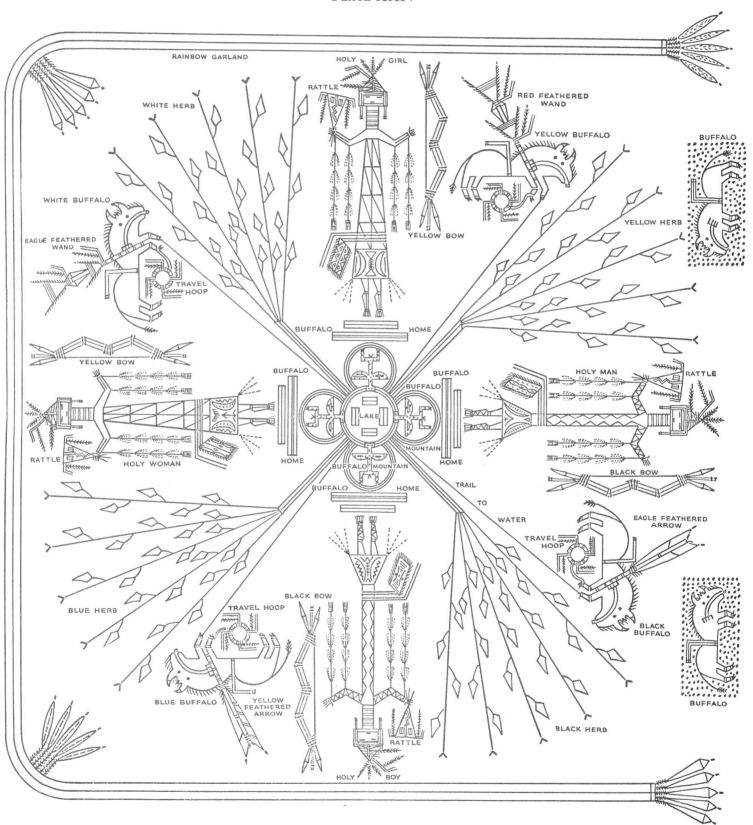

The Buffalo-who-never-dies